COMBAT AIRCRAFT

148 NAKAJIMA Ki-49 'HELEN' UNITS

SERIES EDITOR TONY HOLMES

148

COMBAT AIRCRAFT

George Eleftheriou

NAKAJIMA Ki-49 'HELEN' UNITS

OSPREY
PUBLISHING

OSPREY PUBLISHING

Bloomsbury Publishing Plc

Kemp House, Chawley Park, Cumnor Hill, Oxford OX2 9PH, UK

29 Earlsfort Terrace, Dublin 2, Ireland

1385 Broadway, 5th Floor, New York, NY 10018, USA

E-mail; info@ospreypublishing.com

www.ospreypublishing.com

OSPREY is a trademark of Osprey Publishing Ltd

First published in Great Britain in 2023

A catalogue record for this book is available from the British Library.

ISBN; PB 9781472854490; eBook 9781472854506; ePDF 9781472854476; XML 9781472854483

23 24 25 26 27   10 9 8 7 6 5 4 3 2 1

Edited by Tony Holmes
Cover Artwork by Gareth Hector
Aircraft Profiles by Jim Laurier
Index by Fionbar Lyons
Typeset by PDQ Digital Media Solutions, UK
Printed and bound in India by Replika Press Private Ltd

Osprey Publishing supports the Woodland Trust, the UK's leading woodland conservation charity.

To find out more about our authors and books visit **www.ospreypublishing.com**. Here you will find extracts, author interviews, details of forthcoming events and the option to sign up for our newsletter.

Front Cover

On 27 March 1944, tragedy struck during the very first mission mounted by the 62nd Sentai, newly-equipped with the Ki-49. The target for the day was the starting point of the famous 'Ledo Road' at Assam, in India, along which the Allies provided China with much needed supplies to continue its war effort against Japan. Nine 'Helens' were assigned to the mission, escorted by 60 Ki-43 'Oscar' fighters from the 50th, 64th and 204nd Sentai. However, the opposition they faced was overwhelming. USAAF P-51As, A-36As and P-40Ns scored a clear victory against the Ki-49s and their Ki-43 escorts, with the Japanese formation losing eight bombers and three fighters. In turn, the USAAF lost two P-51s and a P-40. In this specially commissioned cover artwork by Gareth Hector, two of the 'Helens' that fell to the Mustangs' guns can be seen well ablaze after suffering mortal damage.

PREVIOUS PAGES

This 95th Sentai, 2nd Chutai Ki-49 Model 2 Otsu was found wrecked by US Army soldiers at San Manuel, a satellite airfield at the Clark Field complex following the liberation of the latter in February 1945. The red slanting fuselage band immediately forward of the tail was the sentai marking, the bomber lacking the white combat stripe usually found in this location on IJAAF aircraft (*Joe Picarella Collection*)

CONTENTS

CHAPTER ONE

Ki-49 DEVELOPMENT

Throughout the late 1920s and into the early 1930s, the Imperial Japanese Army and Navy sought to update their air fleets by obtaining samples of the latest military aircraft being built internationally, and then either acquiring the production rights or, little by little, experimenting with locally produced designs incorporating aspects of these foreign types. For example, the first all-metal twin-engined Imperial Japanese Army Air Force (IJAAF) bombers were based on the solitary example of a Junkers K 37 that was imported in February 1931. The K 37 became the basis for the design of the Army Type 93 Heavy Bomber (Mitsubishi Ki-1). The first prototype was completed in 1933, and from the spring of 1934 newly produced aircraft started to be delivered to bomber units. A total of 118 Ki-1s were eventually built by Mitsubishi.

The only IJAAF bomber that could objectively earn the title of 'heavy' was also built in 1931. This was the four-engined Type 92 Heavy Bomber (Mitsubishi Ki-20), a licence-built copy of the Junkers G 38 passenger aircraft. The six Ki-20s constructed were each powered by four 750 hp Junkers Jumo 204 six-cylinder, liquid-cooled, opposed-piston diesel engines, and the aircraft could carry a bombload of 5000-kg. The Ki-20 had an empty weight of 15,000-kg and, when fully loaded, weighed an impressive 25,000-kg.

A major breakthrough in the Japanese aviation industry was achieved with the purchase of 12 Douglas DC-2 transports in 1934, followed

An early production Ki-21 'Sally' shares the ramp at an unidentified airfield with a Ki-20 heavy bomber. Only six of the latter were built by Mitsubishi, and since they were underpowered, their engines were constantly upgraded. The type's existence was kept a well-guarded secret, earning it the nickname 'obake' (ghost). The Ki-21, on the other hand, was a modern bomber that signified a breakaway from the influence of German aircraft designs and the espousal of concepts closer to US ideas (*Author's Collection*)

Typical of other bomber designs of its era, the Ki-1 featured an open cockpit and gunner's stations, with the bombload hung beneath the wings (*Author's Collection*)

This DC-2, photographed at Tokyo's Haneda airfield, was the second of six examples built under licence by Nakajima. Given the civilian registration J-BBOO, it was christened *Kirishima* after a mountain in Kyushu and flown by Great Japan Airways. On 15 November 1944, during a flight from Beijing to Fukuoka, the aircraft experienced engine trouble during take-off and crash-landed one kilometre from the airfield (*Author's Collection*)

shortly thereafter by the acquisition of a production licence for the type by Nakajima – six were subsequently built in 1935–37. This gave the company the necessary experience to design its own multi-engined bombers.

In 1937 an extensive re-armament programme was commenced that would ultimately result in the IJAAF fielding aircraft that were on a par with other aeronautically advanced nations. The 'heavy bomber' competition of 1936, which saw Mitsubishi and Nakajima field rival designs as replacements for the Ki-1 and Ki-20, ended with the adoption of the Mitsubishi Ki-21. The winning aircraft (known as the Army Type 97 Heavy Bomber) was largely based on the Nakajima proposal, designated the Ki-19. Indeed, the similarity between the two types resulted in Nakajima being contracted to build Ki-21s.

In early 1938, just as the first examples of the Army Type 97 Heavy Bomber were entering service with the 14th Sentai, the IJAAF issued

the specifications for its next heavy bomber design, which was to be acquired as a replacement for the Ki-21. Responsible for the construction of 351 Mitsubishi bombers (between August 1938 and February 1941), Nakajima was very familiar with the Ki-21's shortcomings – relatively modest range, limited manoeuvrability, a barely adequate top speed and light defensive armament.

The new aircraft, which would receive the designation Ki-49, was intended to operate without fighter escort, relying on its improved speed and heavier armament for protection. Performance parameters stipulated by the IJAAF were a top speed of 311 mph, a range of 1864 miles and an armament of one 20 mm cannon and five 7.7 mm machine guns. Curiously, there was no required increase in the maximum 1000-kg bomb load carried by the Ki-21, although the IJAAF stipulated that armour protection had to be fitted for the six- to eight-man crew and self-sealing fuel tanks were to be installed.

Nakajima's design team for the Ki-49 was led by senior engineer Tei Koyama, who was assisted by three senior engineers – Setsuro Nishimura (who had been assistant designer for the Ki-19), Hideo Itokawa (a fighter design expert) and Iwao Shibuya (fuselage design). In view of the team's previous association with the Ki-19, and its familiarity with the Ki-21, it is unsurprising that the design for the Ki-49 closely resembled both bombers. Like them, it was a mid-wing monoplane of all-metal construction with fabric-covered control surfaces and a low-aspect-ratio wing, the latter being chosen to provide good handling at low to medium altitudes.

A roomy main cockpit and fully glazed nose section were provided to house the pilot and co-pilot (with the latter also doubling as the bombardier), whilst the radio operator sat behind them with his Hi-1 set. Four or five gunners manned defensive armament, which comprised a Type Ho-1 20 mm cannon mounted on a turret ring beneath the aft-facing dorsal step canopy, and single Te-4 7.7 mm machine guns in the nose, port and starboard beam and ventral positions, as well as in the tail turret – the latter was a first for an IJAAF aircraft. Each of the Te-4s featured a 70-round circular magazine, and the weapon was capable of firing 730 rounds per minute. The Ho-1 20 mm anti-tank cannon was fed shells from specially designed 15-round magazines. The Ki-49 could carry 1000-kg of ordnance in a large internal bomb-bay that extended nearly the whole

Nakajima built only two prototypes of the Ki-19, as the aircraft was rejected by the IJAAF in favour of the Ki-21. This example was subsequently purchased by the Domei News Agency following the removal of its military equipment. The aircraft received the civilian registration J-BACN and was nicknamed 'Sakigake' (pioneer) (*Author's Collection*)

Ki-49 Model 1s on the assembly line of Nakajima's Ota factory. Note the rear bracing struts of the landing gear next to the cowling of the port engine. The undercarriage, as with all Japanese bombers built from the 1930s until war's end, was basically a copy of the main gear legs fitted to the DC-2 (*Author's Collection*)

length of the wing chord section, allowing the aircraft to employ a wide range of ordnance of varying sizes.

The original intention was to power the bomber with two 1250 hp Nakajima Ha-41 engines, but as these were not available in time, the first prototype was fitted instead with a pair of 850 hp Nakajima Ha-5 KAI 14-cylinder, air-cooled radial engines driving Hamilton two-pitch, three-bladed propellers. The prototype first flew in August 1939, with Maj Takeshi Yagi (commander of the 61st Sentai) at the controls. Following the construction of two more prototypes (both powered by Ha-41s), an additional seven pre-production aircraft (all fitted with constant-speed propellers) were built in 1940 for a protracted flight trials programme that saw minor modifications made to the armament, crew protection and seating arrangements.

Finally, in March 1941, the aircraft was accepted for production as the Army Type 100 Heavy Bomber Model 1 (Ki-49-I). It was also christened Donryu ('Swallowing Dragon') after a Buddhist temple with the same name located near the Nakajima plant at Ota, in Gunma Prefecture, where the aircraft was built. The Ki-49 would subsequently be given the Allied reporting name 'Helen', as all Japanese bombers, reconnaissance aircraft and flying boats received girls' names in the designation system devised by Capt Frank McCoy of the Material Section, Directorate of Intelligence, Allied Air Forces, Southwest Pacific Area in mid-1942.

The first Ki-49-I rolled off the assembly line at the end of August 1941, and it took a full 12 months to complete the initial order for 128 aircraft. Bombers were rushed into service almost immediately after the completion of the manufacturer's post-production check flights.

Although Ki-49-I crews appreciated having armour protection, self-sealing fuel tanks and good defensive armament, they quickly found that the bomber's engines were unreliable during take-off or at high speeds, when maximum output was required. Furthermore, the Ha-41s only gave the aircraft a marginal performance advantage over the Ki-21, leaving the Ki-49-I vulnerable to interception by enemy fighters. Nakajima duly decided to power the follow-on Ki-49-II with Ha-109 14-cylinder air-cooled radial piston engines rated at 1500 hp each for take-off.

Ki-49 Model 2 Otsu under construction at Ota. Note the windows in the side of the rear fuselage – an identification feature unique to this model (Author's Collection)

Installing the new engines was relatively easy. Although heavier and longer than the Ha-41, the Ha-109's diameters were almost identical. Few modifications to the cowlings and nacelles were needed, although the three slightly broader blades of the new constant-speed propellers were a noticeable feature. The Ha-109 promised to improve the performance of the Ki-49, but Nakajima initially struggled to get hold of examples of the engine. Indeed, it was not until the autumn of 1941 that work started on installing them in two Ki-49-I airframes, and the first of the resulting Ki-49-II prototypes was completed in December 1941. The new variant also incorporated thicker armour for the crew, improved self-sealing tanks and

This photograph of a Ki-49 Model 2 Ko of the Hamamatsu school provides an excellent view of the front of the aircraft, with its many windows and very streamlined fuselage. This particular example was serial number 3032 (Author's Collection)

various internal equipment changes, including a new bombsight. The existing armament was improved slightly in that the ventral Te-4 was replaced by a 7.92 mm Type 100 or Type 1 twin machine gun mounting, and the remaining four by 7.9 mm Type 98s (copies of the German MG 15 machine gun).

Performance tests commenced immediately at Fussa, near Tokyo, and by late spring 1942 plans were made to put the Army Type 100 Heavy Bomber

Donryu serial number 3003 (the very first Ki-49 Model 2 bomber to leave the Ota production line) provides the backdrop for a new graduate of the Hamamatsu school (*Author's Collection*)

Model 2A (Ki-49-IIa) into production. Work commenced on the improved bomber in August of that year, although it was not officially accepted by the IJAAF until June 1943. The Model 2 Ko remained in production virtually unchanged until September 1943, when repeated calls for armament upgrades resulted in the Model 2 Otsu (Ki-49-IIb) that had all the 7.9 mm Type 1 weapons replaced with 12.7mm Ho-103 machine guns. New fuselage beam gun position windows were also added and the bomb aimer's window was altered to give a wider field of view.

There was one other minor, but noticeable, change with the Ki-49-IIb. It would appear that the extra power of the Ha-109 engines had caused overheating problems for the Model 2A. In an effort to overcome this issue with the Model 2 Otsu, the oil cooler was moved from inside the engine cowling to a new position beneath it. Also, on late production models, the engine collector exhaust outlets were replaced by individual exhaust ejectors for each cylinder.

The Army Type 100 Heavy Bomber Model 3 (Ki-49-III), six examples of which were built between March and December 1943, was a further attempt to improve the overall performance of the aircraft through the installation of more powerful Nakajima Ha-107 2400 hp radial engines. These were soon replaced, however, by Nakajima Ha-117s rated at 2600 hp each.

The exact total number of Ki-49s delivered to the IJAAF is not known. Apart from Nakajima, which delivered 746 aircraft (617 of which were Model 2s), Japanese sources mention that Tachikawa Hikoki K.K. also produced as many as 50 Ki-49-IIs over 12 months from January 1943 after the fixing of incorrectly shaped jigs supplied by Nakajima. Although Manshu Hikoki Seizo K.K. was also chosen to build the aircraft, none were completed.

Summary of overall Ki-49 production by Nakajima								
Type	Airframe Nos.	1939	1940	1941	1942	1943	1944	Total
Ki-49 prototypes	4901–4903	3	-	-	-	-	-	3
Ki-49 pre-production	4904–4910	-	7	-	-	-	-	7
Ki-49-I	111–239	-	-	129		-	-	129
Ki-49-II prototypes	3001–3002	-	-	2	-		-	2
Ki-49-II	3003–3604	-	-	-		601		601
Ki-49-III	unknown	-	-	-	-	6	-	6
Total								**748**

VARIANTS

Whilst Ki-49-I service evaluation was in progress, reports from the conflict in China indicated that Ki-21s were suffering higher than anticipated losses because their Nakajima Army Type 97 Fighter (Ki-27) escorts had insufficient range to accompany them all the way to their targets. In an attempt to remedy this situation as expeditiously as possible, the IJAAF sought the provision of a heavily armed, long-range escort fighter to protect the vulnerable flanks of a bomber formation, rather than its front and rear. In order to avoid disrupting Ki-21 production, the new escort fighter requirement was given to Nakajima instead of Mitsubishi.

The company's response was to convert three Ki-49 pre-production aircraft into Ki-58 Army Experimental Escort Fighters, with the work overseen by engineer Kenichi Matsumura. Very early examples of the more powerful 1450 hp Nakajima Ha-109 engine were installed and test flown in the three Ki-58 prototypes. The Ki-49-I's standard armament was increased by the installation of a second top turret, whilst the bomb-bay was sealed and a ventral gondola fitted instead. A single 20 mm Type Ho-1 cannon was installed in each of these new positions, and two more replaced two of the five 7.7 mm Type 89 machine guns, thus bringing the total cannon armament to five – the remaining three 7.7 mm Type 89s were replaced by larger-calibre 12.7mm Type Ho-103 machine guns. This extra firepower resulted in the crew complement being increased from eight to ten or eleven.

The conversions took place between December 1940 and March 1941, but all further work was abandoned when the Nakajima Army Type 1 Fighter Model 1A (Ki-43-Ia) entered service in 1941 and proved itself quite capable of fulfilling the long-range escort requirement.

At around the same time as the Ki-58 concept was being explored, and before the first production Ki-49-Is had been completed (in August 1941), the IJAAF considered a specially armoured version of the aircraft, designated the Ki-80, that would be used exclusively by formation commanders charged with leading Donryu-equipped units into action. Two early production airframes were allocated for this purpose and completed in October 1941. Like the earlier Ki-58s, they were also fitted with Ha-109 engines, as well as a glazed observation position for the commander on top

A rare shot of one of the Ki-58 escort fighter prototypes. The aircraft has a gondola under the centre fuselage and an additional turret aft of the canopy. Behind the Ki-58 is a Douglas A-20 that had been captured in Java and brought back to Japan for evaluation (*Author's Collection*)

Donryu take part in the annual military parade on 29 April to mark the Emperor's birthday. This photograph was probably taken in 1943. The 'Helen' in the foreground belongs to the Hamamatsu school, the one at top right is an aircraft from the Radio Operator's School and the Ki-49 in the middle was assigned to the Army Air Academy (*Author's Collection*)

of the fuselage and a ventral gondola. Flight testing quickly revealed that the added weight of the armour made the Ki-80 appreciably slower than a standard Ki-49-I, so this idea was also abandoned.

UNIT STRUCTURE

Ki-49-Is started reaching the IJAAF in late August 1941, joining a growing bomber force that could trace its lineage back to the establishment of the 7th Rentai (regiment) on 1 May 1925 with aircraft and crews from the Tachikawa-based 5th Rentai. Initially consisting of only one chutai (flight), the 7th Rentai had three more established by January 1930, although only two of them were equipped with 12 Type 87 Night Bombers apiece as the 1st Daitai (battalion). The remaining two chutai each flew nine Type 88 Light Bombers as the 2nd Daitai. At that time regiments often included flights equipped with different types of aircraft.

When the Second Sino-Japanese War commenced on 7 July 1937, the IJAAF comprised 52 chutai – 19 fighter, 13 reconnaissance, 11 heavy bomber and nine light bomber. In the second half of the following year, the IJAAF underwent a major reorganisation. Rentai were simply too large when they included fighter, reconnaissance and bomber battalions, causing numerous supply and transportation problems. These issues were exacerbated by the inclusion of support battalions charged with, for example, the supply of ammunition and provisions, as well as the maintenance and guarding of airfields. All this changed under the 'Air and Ground Separation Plan'.

The air combat divisions were separated from airfield battalions, the former now organised into sentai (equivalent to a group or wing in other contemporary air forces) with a headquarters and two to three more chutai (squadrons or companies) all usually flying a single type of aircraft.

When Japan attacked the Allies in December 1941, the IJAAF could field eight heavy bomber sentai, all equipped with Ki-21-I/IIs. Most of these units had gained invaluable experience with the aircraft during the Second Sino-Japanese War, allowing crews to perfect their offensive and defensive techniques. During the first six months of the Pacific War, the Ki-21-equipped units greatly assisted the lightning advance of the ground forces in the Philippines, Malaya and Burma.

The Ki-21 sentai (the majority of which later switched to the Ki-49) were manned by crews that had graduated from the IJAAF's main heavy bomber school at Hamamatsu, in Shizuoka Prefecture. It had been established on 1 August

A classic photograph featuring an unpainted Model 1 'Helen' from the Hamamatsu school flying in front of Mount Fuji (*Author's Collection*)

1933, and from 1941 offered two courses – a three-month course for NCOs and lower rank officers, and a six-month course for captains and higher rank officers. The former became the main pilots of the bomber crews. They sat on the left side of the cockpit and operated the aircraft during take-off, landing and formation flight. The latter became the commanders, co-pilots and bombardiers of the aircraft. When Japanese sources mention 'X's bomber', they always refer to the co-pilot/commander of the aircraft sat in the right seat, not the lower rank main pilot to his left.

During group bombing missions, the mission commander would fly with the aircraft leading the formation. Immediately prior to commencing the bombing run on the target, he would leave the cockpit and move to the front of the aircraft in order to operate the aiming device. The co-pilots of the following bombers would remain in their seats and pay very close attention to the leader's aircraft. The exact moment he released his bombs, they would too (the co-pilot could release the bombs from the cockpit). When flying individually, during night bombing missions for example, the co-pilot of each bomber would move to the nose and release the bombs whenever he saw fit.

A typical jubakutai (heavy bomber unit) formation in full chutai force would include three hentai (flights) of three or four bombers each flying in a 'wedge' ('flying V') configuration. The bomber at the tip of the 'V' would be the lead aircraft (No 1), with the one on the right being its No 2 and the one on the left its No 3, while the fourth aircraft slotted in behind the No 2. The three hentai would fly in a similar pattern, with the first bomber leading the formation, the second flying behind and to the right of it and the third off to the left side of the formation. In reality, IJAAF heavy bomber sentai (primarily equipped with Ki-49s) that saw action after the second half of 1943 seldom flew missions involving more than six aircraft. These were divided into two hentai of three aircraft each, with

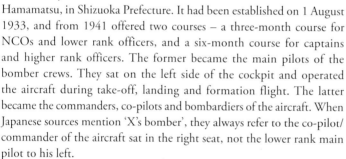

Aircrew in a hentai of Hamamatsu 'Helens' are trained to fly in wedge formation – a tactic used by IJAAF heavy bomber units in daylight operations throughout World War 2 (*Author's Collection*)

a mix of bombers from different chutai depending on how many were in an airworthy condition at the time.

Crews communicated either by radio or the flight signal system, the latter consisting of three red, yellow and blue translucent panels (each of which contained an electric lamp) housed at the rear of the cockpit. When the formation commander wanted to signal the other aircraft, he raised a combination of these panels. For example, a raised red and yellow panel meant 'assume combat formation'.

IJAAF heavy bomber crews were taught two ways to approach a target. During the first, the aircraft flew directly over the target and released its bombload, before making a 180-degree turn and setting course for home. Although such an attack profile gave bomber crews the element of surprise, it also meant that if the enemy was forewarned by radar or lookout stations, allowing the scrambling of defending fighters, the latter

A closer in-flight photograph of a group of Hamamatsu school Donryu, all of which are factory-fresh early production examples lacking armament. Unusually, the Type was the first and only Japanese aircraft to have the fuselage door on the starboard side (*Author's Collection*)

would have enough time to attack the bombers during the slow turn and second pass over the target as they headed for home. Anti-aircraft fire would also be able to engage the bombers for an extended length of time during this period. Most missions where IJAAF bomber units suffered heavy casualties were as a result of crews choosing this method of attack.

The second attack profile saw the bomber formation fly some distance from the target before the aircraft turned and then attacked while already heading in the direction of home. As this profile gave defending forces much less time to engage the attacking bombers, it was the method most favoured by crews.

For the majority of bombing missions Ki-49s were loaded with 50-kg bombs, and very occasionally with a combination of 50- and 100-kg bombs. The aircraft carried 250-kg bombs only when targeting ships, and many crews received special training in skip bombing for such attacks. Ki-49s only carried 500-kg bombs when the aircraft were assigned suicide missions in the final months of the war, the crew being expected to slam into an enemy vessel. Typically, bombs would be released from altitudes between 3000 and 6000 m. Attacks from lower altitudes were undertaken during night missions when, in many cases, the bombers were loaded with 30- or 50-kg Ta-Dan cluster bombs.

Although the 'Helens' of the Hamamatsu school were initially flown unpainted, from 1944, and especially after the fall of Saipan and the commencement of USAAF heavy bomber raids on Japan, all examples were hastily camouflaged. The rather limiting and complex system of identification bands that had previously been used by the unit's Ki-49s was also replaced at this time by an individual aircraft number applied on the tail immediately beneath the school marking (*Author's Collection*)

This Donryu of the Rikugun Koku Seibi Gakko (Army Aircraft Maintenance School) has had its Fowler flaps and undercarriage extended in preparation for landing. The school was founded at Tokorozawa, in Saitama Prefecture, on 1 July 1938, and it was responsible for instructing students on aircraft maintenance and handling, repair theory and practise and logistical support. A number of frontline and training types were available for the students to practice on, including examples of the 'Helen' bomber (*Author's Collection*)

A Model 1 'Helen' of the *Rikugun Koku Tsushin Gakko* (Army Flight Radio Operators School) is seen on the flightline of the Hamamatsu school during a visit to the airfield. The school was formed at Mito, in Ibaraki Prefecture, in August 1940, from where it operated a mix of aircraft types and trained all IJAAF radio operators (*Author's Collection*)

Comparative data table of Ki-49 with bombers of similar size and era						
	Ki-21-II	**G4M1**	**Ki-49-II**	**Wellington IC**	**He 111H-6**	**B-25C Mitchell**
Empty weight	6015-kg	6800-kg	6530-kg	8459-kg	8680-kg	8840-kg
Max weight	9523-kg	9500-kg	10,680-kg	13,381-kg	12,030-kg	15,200-kg
Engine output (take-off)	1410 hp	1530 hp	1450 hp	1050 hp	1300 hp	1700 hp
Max speed	478 km/h	428 km/h	492 km/h	377 km/h	440 km/h	438 km/h
Range	2400 km	6030 km	2950 km	3540 km	2300 km	2050 km
Service ceiling	10,000 m	8534 m	9300 m	5486 m	6500 m	7400 m
Bombload	1000-kg	1000-kg	750–1000-kg	2041-kg	2000-kg	1800-kg

This Model 2 Otsu was assigned to the obscure 105th Kyoiku Hiko Rentai (105th Training Flight Regiment), which had been organised on 30 September 1941 at Hamamatsu. In August 1942, one of its chutai was transferred to the newly formed 116th Kyoiku Hiko Rentai. On 31 March 1944, the unit changed its name to the 5th Kyoiku Hikotai (Training Flight Unit) (*Author's collection*)

Ki-49 comparative specifications			
	Ki-49-I (prototype)	**Ki-49-I (production)**	**Ki-49-II (production)**
Army Type 100	heavy bomber	heavy bomber	heavy bomber
Crew	6	8	8
Engine type	Nakajima Ha-5 Kai	Nakajima Ha-41	Nakajima Ha-109
Engine output	850 hp	1250 hp	1450 hp
Wingspan	20.4 m	20.4 m	20.4 m
Length	16.8 m	16.5 m	16.5 m
Height	4.25 m	4.25 m	4.25 m
Wing area	69.05 m²	69.05 m²	69.05 m²
Weight empty	–	6070-kg	6530-kg
Weight loaded	–	10,150-kg	10,680-kg
Wing loading	–	147-kg/m²	154.7-kg/m²
Power loading	–	4.1-kg/hp)	3.6-kg/hp
Maximum speed	–	–	492 km/h
Time to climb	–	–	5000 m in 13 min 39 sec
Service ceiling	–	–	9300 m
Range	–	–	2950 km

CHAPTER TWO

DARWIN AND NEW GUINEA

The first frontline units to swap their Ki-21s for Ki-49s were the 7th and 61st Sentai. The 7th had been formed on 31 August 1938 and the 61st (based at Chichihar, in Manchuria) on 1 September. The former had received its first Ki-21s in the summer of 1939 while based at Hamamatsu. It was relocated to Gongzhuling, in Jilin Province, in June 1941 as a reserve unit charged with the defence of Manchuria. In July–August 1942 the 7th swapped its Ki-21-IIs for Ki-49-Is, after which all crews received extensive tuition in long-distance navigation. By the end of August, the unit was capable of fly distances of more than 1000 km – no mean feat for an IJAAF heavy bomber crew.

The 7th, together with the 61st Sentai, comprised the 9th Hikodan (Air Brigade). In August 1942, the brigade became part of the 3rd Kokugun (Air Army), headquartered in Singapore, and was assigned to maritime patrol duties on the South Front. The 7th, with 22 bombers and six reserve aircraft, and the 61st left Manchuria on 12 September, and after engine failures and many stops at airfields in China, Taiwan and Vietnam, finally reached their bases of operation on 3 October. The 7th Sentai called Kalijati airfield, in west Java (present-day Suryadarma AFB), home, while the 61st Sentai was assigned to Medan, in northern Sumatra.

Until May 1943, the units undertook reconnaissance missions over Sumatra and Java and anti-submarine patrols over the Indian Ocean. A handful of bombing raids were also mounted against the remote

Groundcrew attend to the starboard engine of a Ki-49 Model 2 Otsu from the 7th Sentai prior to the aircraft undertaking another mission in the summer of 1943 (*Author's Collection*)

Christmas and Cocos Islands. On 18 May, most of the Ki-49-Is assigned to the 3rd Kokugun were transferred from Kalijati to Kakamigahara airfield, in Gifu Prefecture, where crews received new Model 2s from the Utsunomiya aviation arsenal. In late May the unit's forward echelons returned to the South Front, arriving in Singapore. By 9 June, both the 7th and 61st Sentai were classified as being combat ready.

DARWIN

The port of Darwin, in Australia's Northern Territory, had been an important hub in the US South Pacific air ferry route prior to the start of the Pacific War. Bomber reinforcements bound for the US Army Air Corps (USAAC) in the Philippines would stop over here to avoid flightpaths through the Japanese mandates in the central Pacific. Following the outbreak of fighting in-theatre, and the rapid advance of Japanese forces in Malaya, Darwin became a key Allied base in the defence of the Netherlands East-Indies (NEI). From its harbour, vessels carrying both men and materiel headed for the NEI, and then returned carrying Dutch civilians that had been evacuated in the face of Japanese advances.

The Imperial Japanese Army (IJA) had scheduled landings on Timor for February 1942, and a full invasion of Java was to take place shortly thereafter. In order to protect these landings from Allied interference, the Japanese military command mounted a devastating air raid on Darwin on 19 February involving 188 Imperial Japanese Naval Air Force (IJNAF) aircraft launched from four carriers.

Later that same day, IJA troops landed in Timor, where they met resistance from a small Allied force that commenced guerrilla warfare in a campaign lasting until their final evacuation in February 1943. They were resupplied by aircraft and vessels based mostly in Darwin. The Japanese, fearful that raids could be conducted against Timor or other significant island bases in the NEI, decided to begin a bombing campaign against Darwin that would continue until November 1943, resulting in more than 260 deaths. A total of 97 raids targeted Darwin in that time, with all bar one of them being undertaken by the IJNAF.

In May 1943, the 9th Hikodan received orders to prepare for an attack on northern Australia. The 61st Sentai immediately started training in the use of oxygen for high-altitude operations, as well as perfecting its formation bombing from 7000 m. On 13 June, the 61st Sentai was reassigned to the 3rd Hikodan, which included the 59th Sentai equipped with 22 Ki-43 'Oscar' fighters, the 75th Sentai with nine Ki-48 'Lily' light bombers and the 70th Dokuritsu Hiko Chutai

A Model 1 'Helen' of the 61st Sentai is loaded with 15 50-kg bombs at Lautem in the early morning hours of 20 June 1943, immediately prior to participating in the raid on Winnellie airfield and the nearby Frances Bay explosives depot (*Author's Collection*)

(Independent Squadron), which would reconnoitre the target and observe the results of the raid with its Ki-46 'Dinah' reconnaissance aircraft.

The commander of the 61st, Lt Col Takeshi Yagi (who, as previously mentioned, had test flown the first Donryu prototype) issued the following orders on 15 June;

'1) Target – Enemy aircraft and facilities at Port Darwin airfield [Winnellie airfield].

'2) Date and time – 20 June at 0930 hrs.

'3) Number of aircraft – six from each chutai, 18 in total.

'4) Formation – Standard cruising formation. 2nd Chutai in the lead, 1st Chutai on the right side and 3rd Chutai on the left.

'5) Altitude – Cruising altitude will be 5700 m. After entering the bombing run, aircraft will slowly descend to 5000 m and release the bombload.

'6) Bombload – 15 x 50-kg bombs, fitted with short-delay fuses, for each aircraft.

'7) Departure will be from Lautem airfield. However, in order to conceal our objective, each chutai will relocate to Lautem independently, on 16, 17 and 18 June. Special consideration should be given to the accommodation of the aircraft and crews [Lautem was a secret airfield, difficult to spot from the air, with only minimal facilities. It was mainly used as a staging base, as in this case, or for emergency landings].

'8) The sentai commander will fly in the leading aeroplane and will be in charge of the formation.'

The sentai commander in the lead bomber was Capt Toshio Miyazawa, who had been part of the crew of a Ki-46 'Dinah' that had carried out a reconnaissance and photography mission over Darwin at an altitude of 9500 m on 17 June. This sortie had confirmed the absence of enemy aircraft at Winnellie and the exact location of the main facilities to be attacked. The Ki-46 had been opposed by anti-aircraft batteries at Fannie Bay, McMillans and Berrimah.

Following the original plan, all the chutai of the 61st had assembled a force of 21 aircraft (including three reserve bombers) at Lautem by 19 June. The following day, the crews got up at 0400 hrs, travelled to their Ki-49s an hour later and, after careful equipment inspection and engine test runs, gathered in front of the battle command post at 0600 hrs. Each chutai commander addressed the crews under his command, and the words of Capt Katsuhiro Ohta, 1st Chutai commander, were recorded in the 61st's official unit history;

'We will form a tight formation to attack and strike a meticulous blow to the enemy. If you are unlucky and get hit by enemy fire or suffer engine or other mechanical failure, you should do your utmost to return to base. But if you judge that this is impossible, don't let your sacrifice go to waste. Try to hit an enemy aircraft or enemy airfield facilities. In any case, this should be done only as a last resort.'

At 0630 hrs the crews boarded their aircraft, and ten minutes later a small white flag fluttered from the canopy of Capt Miyazawa's bomber and the 2nd Chutai started taking off, followed by the 1st and the 3rd. Meanwhile, the maintenance personnel had lined up on the side of the runway to wave the crews goodbye.

The engines of a 61st Sentai 'Helen' are test run before the bomber heads off for Darwin. Note that two of the aircrew in the foreground are wearing IJNAF-issue life jackets – a sensible precaution in light of the fact that much of the 1500-km round trip to Darwin would be spent over water (*Author's Collection*)

Once airborne, the Ki-49s were joined by 22 Ki-43s of the 59th Sentai, led by unit CO Maj Takeo Fukuda, and nine Ki-48s of the 75th Sentai, led by Capt Wataru Komazawa – the latter aircraft were also based at Lautem. Soon, all 18 'Helens' had taken their place within the formation, which continued to slowly climb before turning to the south and crossing the 650 km of the Arafura Sea to Darwin. After passing the northern end of Bathurst Island, and about 100 km north of Darwin, the 1st Chutai's aircraft No 4, flown by Lt Kuwahara, signalled that it had engine trouble and left the formation to return to Lautem.

At 0930 hrs, just when the leading bombers were about to make a right turn and head for Darwin, 37 Spitfires of the Royal Australian Air Force's No 1 Fighter Wing attacked from an altitude of 2000 m. 38 Radar Station at Cape Fourcroy, on Bathurst Island, had detected the Japanese aircraft and the Spitfires had been scrambled in response. The Ki-43s in turn attempted to engage the RAAF fighters. However, a number of Spitfires succeeded in attacking the 1st Chutai from the lower right side, and a burst from the fighter flown by Flg Off John Bisley hit the starboard engine of Capt Ohta's lead bomber, setting it on fire.

The Ki-49 soon slowed, and it was unable to keep up with the formation. Despite the crew's best efforts, the fire could not be controlled. According to Lt Natomi from the 1st Chutai, Ohta 'bid farewell to his companion aircraft from amidst the rising smoke, [and] with a white handkerchief fluttering, his bomber was observed making a wide roll-over onto an anti-aircraft position on the north side of the [Darwin] air base'. In reality, the Ki-49 crashed on Koolpinyah Station. The bomber of Capt Suzuki quickly took Ohta's place, leading the right echelon of the formation.

Another group of Spitfires attacked from directly above the leading chutai, and Flg Off Tony Hughes and Sqn Ldr Ron MacDonald (CO of No 452 Sqn) targeted Ki-49 No 4 of the 2nd Chutai flown by Lt Kenjiro Matsuhara. They both hit the bomber, which soon began trailing black smoke from the wing fuel tanks as a fierce fire wrapped the entire fuselage.

According to Natomi, Matsuhara's Ki-49 rocked its wings and left the formation after the pilot 'decided to crash into an enemy installation. He went down near Capt Ohta's aeroplane, not far from anti-aircraft sites'. The bomber did in fact crash into Adam Bay.

Aircraft No 5 from the 1st Chutai, flown by Lt Kawamura, was also hit by dozens of rounds in the wing fuel tanks and starboard engine, leaving fuel trailing some five to eight metres behind the wing. Fortunately for the crew, there was no fire, and the bomber was able to keep its position within the formation.

Aircrew from the 61st Sentai receive a warm welcome upon their return to Lautem, having completed a particularly dangerous mission. Unlike their IJNAF counterparts, IJAAF pilots and navigators were not trained to fly over the large expanses of the Pacific and Indian Oceans, so the one-off Ki-49 raid against Darwin was considered a significant accomplishment at the time. Note the Hitachi fuel truck in the background getting into position to refuel the Donryu behind it (*Author's Collection*)

Despite the best efforts of the RAAF Spitfires, the surviving Ki-49s remained on course for their targets in Darwin – Winnellie airfield and the nearby Frances Bay explosives depot. Some 30–40 km from Winnellie, the fighters broke off their attacks and the anti-aircraft batteries took over. Aircraft No 6 of the 1st Chutai, flown by WO Nemoto, received a direct hit that completely obliterated the hinomaru from the underside of its right wing. No RAAF fighters were encountered over the airfield, and the Ki-49s released their ordnance, hitting huts and hangars and starting fires at two locations when 60 oil drums were set alight. The 'Helens' then left the target area in a slow right turn, having been engaged continuously by anti-aircraft batteries. No further damage was inflicted on the bombers, however.

With its starboard engine having been riddled by bullets, Kawamura's aircraft was unable to keep up with the formation as it headed for home. A small number of Spitfires attempted to attack the straggling bomber, but Ki-43 escorts managed to repel them. The crew subsequently had to dump all non-vital equipment in an attempt to lighten the bomber, but when the engine finally seized, reaching Lautem was no longer an option. Kawamura instead headed for Abisu airfield, in East Timor, where he performed a textbook belly landing. Three other bombers that had received lighter damage returned directly to Lautem. The Ki-49s that were in flyable condition were quickly refuelled and then flown out to other airfields, as the 3rd Hikodan feared an enemy counter-attack. Fortunately, that did not materialise.

The Ki-43 pilots and Ki-49 gunners claimed no fewer than 27 Spitfires shot down for the loss of two bombers and a fighter. Three Ki-48s also suffered serious damage, with two crash-landing on Timor and a third on Selaru airfield, in the Tanimbar Islands. The Spitfire pilots claimed eight heavy bombers, one light bomber and five fighters destroyed. Nine bombers and two fighters were also claimed as damaged. No 1 Fighter Wing suffered two losses, with both pilots being killed, and a third Spitfire was destroyed in a landing accident. During the attack on the airfield and the explosives depot, two were killed and 13 wounded.

Ki-49s would never return to Australian skies.

NEW GUINEA

In 1942 the IJA was unstoppable during its advance along the east coast of New Guinea, reaching as far south as Buna, just 100 miles northeast of Port Moresby. However, the failure of Japanese troops to successfully transport heavy weapons and equipment across the near-impenetrable Owen Stanley Range ultimately saved Port Moresby from capture.

The first IJAAF heavy bomber unit in-theatre was the Ki-21-equipped 14th Sentai, which was transferred to Rapopo, near Rabaul, from Malang, in Java, in late February 1943. Its arrival was prompted by the IJNAF being tasked with supporting the faltering campaign in the Solomons, leaving the IJAAF with the responsibility of taking over aerial operations in New Guinea. In August 1943 the 4th Kokugun was formed in response to the massive increase in Allied air power in the region. Amongst the units assigned to it were the 7th and 61st Sentai of the 9th Hikodan, which had previously been based at Surabaya, in east Java.

The 7th Sentai was the first IJAAF heavy bomber unit to be based in New Guinea, its primary missions being to support ground units that had concentrated their efforts against Port Moresby and to counter the threat posed by Allied air forces through the targeting of newly captured or constructed airfields. The unit had been undertaking conversion training onto the Ki-49-II at Hamamatsu when, on 19 June 1943, the 7th Sentai unexpectedly received orders transferring it to Wewak, on the northern New Guinea coast. The unit commander initially questioned the deployment due to the poor state of the airfields in-theatre, stating that they were unsuitable for heavy bombers.

Nevertheless, 35 Ki-49-IIs were shipped to west Java, where they were reassembled at Kalijati airfield in July. On the 20th of that month, the 7th Sentai departed for But East airfield (known to the Allies as Dagua) under the command of new CO, Maj Ohnishi Toyokichi. The first bombers reached But East four days later, having routed via Surabaya, Lautem, Babo, on Celebes Island, and Hollandia. The crews immediately commenced maintenance work on each bomber, concealed fuel, ammunition and equipment and built barracks out of palm trees for the headquarters and each chutai. Ki-49s were first spotted by an Allied reconnaissance aircraft

With its bomb-bay doors open, a Ki-49 Model 2 Otsu from the 7th Sentai awaits the arrival of ordnance at an airfield in northeast New Guinea. Smaller 50-kg bombs were commonly used for missions against enemy airfields, with 100-kg weapons typically employed against shipping. Heavier ordnance of 250-kg was reserved for fortifications, and was rarely used in New Guinea (*Author's Collection*)

on 31 July when 14 were photographed at But East. By mid-August, 20 of the 35 'Helens' sent to Kalijati for the 7th Sentai had reach the airfield.

Following its attack on Darwin, the 61st Sentai departed Surabaya in early August for the airfield on Wakde Island, off the northwestern coast of New Guinea. The coral-surfaced runway was 2200 m long and 70 m wide and it was surrounded by palm trees, between which the Ki-49s could be hidden and maintained. The unit also used But West airfield as a forward base.

While the 61st was settling in at Wakde, the 7th Sentai flew its first mission on 12 August against Mount Hagen airfield in the New Guinea highlands, where the IJAAF believed a major Allied base was being developed. Twenty Ki-49s, escorted by an identical number of Ki-43s from the 59th Sentai, were despatched, and it took the 7th Sentai more than 30 minutes to get its bombers into the air because the runway at But East was too narrow and in poor condition. Once aloft, the pilots struggled to cross the 3000 m high cordillera of the Hagen Mountain range, which were covered in clouds.

The bomber crews were particularly focused on not losing their escorts, but the presence of the latter ultimately proved to be unnecessary, for when the Ki-49s reached Mount Hagen airfield there was no enemy opposition and no aircraft to be seen. All the Donryu released their bombs accurately on the target, and at the end of this uneventful first combat mission they safely returned to base.

Two days later, another formation of seven 'Helens' from the 7th bombed enemy artillery positions near Wau and Lake Salus in joint attacks with IJA ground forces. Again, all the aircraft involved returned to base without any mishaps. On 15 August, seven 'Helens' targeted the recently discovered Fabua airfield (known to the Allies as Tsili Tsili), and the following night three bombers attacked the new USAAF base at Marilinan. Although the crews involved reported seeing considerable secondary explosions, the 7th also suffered its first loss when a Ki-49 failed to return.

On 17 August, the first in a series of low-level bombing and strafing raids on major IJAAF airfields in the Wewak area was conducted by field-modified B-25 Mitchells of the USAAF's Fifth Air Force in preparation for the Allied landings on Lae. But East was hit hard, with 14 Ki-49s being destroyed. Only three bombers managed to take off on a retaliatory night raid against Fabua that evening, although all three crews claimed to have achieved notable results. By the following day the 7th had only four bombers in flyable condition from the 20 originally at But East. On 22 August two of the Ki-49s performed another night raid on Fabua, setting fires in two locations. On the way back, the aircraft fought of an attack by a single-engined fighter.

On 28 August, the Imperial Japanese Navy (IJN) convoy Wewak No 7, which included the transport vessels *Nagato Maru*, *Nagano Maru*, *Hankow Maru*, *Aden Maru* and *Shinyu Maru* loaded with troops and much needed supplies, sailed from Palau bound for the Wewak area. The 7th Sentai sortied its few remaining bombers as convoy escorts, the aircraft also undertaking anti-submarine patrols. Thanks in part to the efforts of the Ki-49 crews, all the transports safely reached Wewak harbour and Boram Bay from 0145 hrs on 2 September and immediately offloaded their

A Ki-49 nose gunner mans a Te-4 weapon. It was equipped with eight magazines containing a total of 544 rounds. The forward clear section of the nose could rotate through 360 degrees, allowing well-trained gunners to provide the bomber with fairly adequate defence thanks to this wide field of fire. In contrast, German and Allied bombers that lacked a dedicated nose turret had to install multiple machine guns to cover a similar field of fire (*Author's Collection*)

supplies. The following morning the vessels were attacked by 30 B-25Ds, escorted by P-38 Lightning fighters. *Nagato Maru* and *Hankow Maru* were sunk and *Nagano Maru* and *Aden Maru* damaged.

On 4 September, the Allied offensive against Lae commenced when the Australian Army's 9th Division made an amphibious landing at Hopoi, on the northern coast of New Guinea. At 2100 hrs that night, two pairs of 'Helens' attacked the landing area and bombed an HQ building and depot, setting them on fire. Despite being intercepted by enemy fighters during the return flight to But East, all four Ki-49s made it back. One aircraft was damaged when landing, and two crewmen, WO Toraji Iwabuchi and Sgt Maj Kenji Watanabe, were killed by fire from the Allied fighters. Another raid by three bombers targeted Hopoi the following evening, and crews reported starting a fire at one location. However, all three aircraft were damaged when landing at But East due to the poor condition of the runway.

The evening of 6 September saw the 61st Sentai make its combat debut in-theatre following the arrival of an advanced detachment at But East from Wakde. The unit sortied two 'Helens' alongside two bombers from the 7th Sentai in a repeat attack on the Hopoi beachhead, but with unknown results. One 61st Sentai bomber failed to return. A final raid on Hopoi was launched during daylight hours on the 8th, with eight bombers from the 7th and the 61st Sentai being escorted by 22 fighters. The crews reported positive results, and all aircraft returned without any mishaps.

Three days later, the headquarters of the 7th Hikoshidan (Flying Division) decided to attack Fabua airfield in a show of force with all the aircraft under its command. Only 12 'Helens' from the 7th and 61st Sentai could be made serviceable from the 15 at But East, and they were escorted by a formidable force of 45 Ki-43 'Oscar' and Ki-61 'Tony' fighters. When the IJAAF formation reached the target, crews discovered that most of the Allied aircraft previously at Fabua had evacuated the area after receiving advanced warning of the raid. The few remaining enemy fighters that scrambled to intercept the Ki-49s were engaged in fierce aerial combat with their escorts, while the bombers had a free hand to release their payload on the airfield facilities. IJAAF fighter pilots claimed no fewer than seven P-38s shot down, while four bombers were damaged during crash-landings upon their return to But East.

Despite the IJAAF HQ in Japan having earmarked Port Moresby as a priority target for the Ki-49s of the 7th Hikoshidan, it was attacked just once by the Donryu. The first such raid was planned for the night of 18 September, but it had to be postponed 48 hours due to bad weather. Finally, shortly after nightfall on the 20th, four 'Helens' from the 7th and

61st Sentai took off from But East in heavy rain. The two aircraft from the 61st failed to clear the 4000 m peaks of the Owen Stanley Range due to the stormy conditions, so they attacked Fabua airfield instead. One of the Ki-49s subsequently ditched off Wewak and the entire crew was lost.

The two bombers from the 7th Sentai, flown by Lt Sakura Toyo'o and WO Ikejima Jushiro, managed to reach Port Moresby, where they came under heavy anti-aircraft fire. Releasing their bombs overhead Allied airfields at 0300 hrs, the crews could not observe the results of their attack because the target area was obscured by cloud cover.

FINSCHHAFEN

Following the rapid capture of Lae on 15 September during the climax of the Lae–Salamaua campaign, the Allies decided to remain on the offensive and launch the Huon Peninsula campaign with an amphibious attack on the strategically important Japanese base at Finschhafen. The 4th Kokugun had anticipated this development, but it lacked conclusive information regarding the date and location of the impending attack. While keeping a watchful eye on the Lae–Salamaua area, the IJAAF decided to press on with its scheduled air raids.

The Allies, meanwhile, planned to assemble an adequate number of landing craft and escorting destroyers in Milne Bay and Buna by 20 September, load the troops at Lae the following day and land at Finschhafen early in the morning of 22 September. On the 20th, an IJAAF reconnaissance aircraft spotted 100+ enemy vessels in the Buna area. Following the receipt of this intelligence, the commander of the 4th Kokugun, Lt Gen Kumaichi Teramoto, ordered the 6th and 7th Hikoshidan to be ready to attack the enemy vessels.

Meanwhile, the 6th Hikoshidan had already planned an attack against Fabua airfield on the 21st, and the 7th Hikoshidan had scheduled another night raid on Port Moresby. Since Teramoto did not yet know the exact intention of the enemy fleet, he decided to plan his course of action after receiving early morning reconnaissance reports on 21 September. At 0800 hrs, nine Ki-21s of the 14th Sentai and 25 fighter escorts duly gathered over Wewak and headed to Fabua.

At about the same time, the Allied landing force that was making its way around the Huon Peninsula bound for Finschhafen was spotted by IJAAF reconnaissance aircraft. Urgent efforts to contact the 6th Hikoshidan formation came to naught, and the bombers stayed on their course. Fabua was covered in cloud, forcing the 'Sally' crews to release their bombs without any chance of confirming the results before heading back to base.

With the 6th Hikoshidan aircraft having expended their ordnance, the 7th Hikoshidan was ordered to attack the Allied ships. Its commander, Lt Gen Einosuke Sudo, wisely requested a fighter escort, but none would be available until the aircraft that had escorted the 6th Hikoshidan during its attack on Fabua had returned to base and been refuelled and rearmed. This meant that the nine Ki-49s of the 7th Sentai tasked with attacking the Allied ships had to wait until 13 Ki-43s from the 24th and 59th Sentai and ten Ki-61s from the 68th and 78th Sentai had been made mission ready once again. Finally, at 1445 hrs, the Ki-49s met up with their escorts over Wewak.

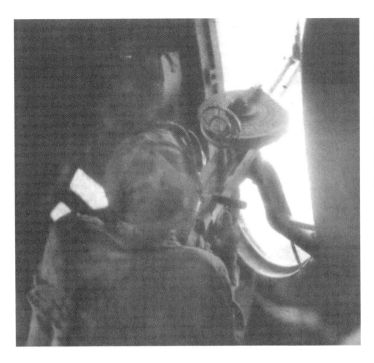

A rare photograph of a Donryu waist gunner in action. There were only four spare magazines containing a total of 408 rounds for the single Te-4 machine guns on the port and starboard sides. Depending on the mission and the necessary combination of fuel, bombload and crew, 'Helens' flew with either one very busy waist gunner who operated both side machine guns or, if there was a sufficient weight allowance, two (*Author's Collection*)

During the course of the day IJAAF reconnaissance aircraft had reported more enemy ships east of Salamaua and south of Hopoi. The 'Helens' found the Allied vessels 15 km east of Hopoi at 1645 hrs and immediately attacked them. WO Keiichi Okawa was the main pilot of one of the Ki-49s that took part in the mission, and he subsequently recalled;

'On 21 September our sentai received orders to attack and destroy the enemy convoy at Markham Bay [off Lae]. Each chutai prepared three aircraft and we all set out in a nine-bomber formation, taking off from But airfield at around 1500 hrs. The escort fighters accompanied us. I was the main pilot of the second aircraft in the 2nd hentai of the 2nd Chutai, and the commander of our bomber was 1Lt Okamoto.

'After take-off, we climbed and flew straight towards Markham Bay, flying at an altitude of 6000 m. We located our target – the enemy fleet – almost immediately. The reconnaissance aircraft had reported that the fleet was protected by a strong escort force. The sky above the target was partly covered by cumulus clouds, and the fleet was appearing and disappearing behind them. Perhaps the hentai commander wasn't able to spot the enemy fleet because he started descending while making a 180-degree turn to the left.

'The anti-aircraft fire from the fleet was intense, and the smoke from the explosions looked like black clouds. The blasts kept shaking the aircraft. We passed over the fleet safely, flew under the clouds and entered the bombing run at an altitude of 4000 m. Dozens of "Grumman" fighters [while all US pilots thought Japanese fighters were "Zeros", to Japanese airmen, especially bomber crews, all enemy fighters were "Grummans"], probably from an aircraft carrier, were waiting under the clouds. They attacked us from the front in a three-aircraft formation, all of them shooting at the same time. Their tracers looked like fireworks. When an enemy fighter looked like a bean grain, all the tracers seemed like they were hitting you, but actually they were passing all over and around you.

'Our gunners started shooting back and our escort fighters became embroiled in fierce aerial battles. At the same time, immense anti-aircraft fire came from the enemy ships. We knew that if we broke formation, we would be picked out and mercilessly attacked, so we did everything we could to stay in our battle formation.

'Suddenly, a bullet hit the windscreen. I felt like I had been punched in the face and everything went pitch black for a moment. I wiped my face with my right hand and discovered that my glove was filled with blood, which was running down my neck. There was a big hole in the windscreen and a strong wind was blowing through it, making the aircraft difficult to control, but I said to myself, "There is no way I'm getting shot down like that", and desperately stayed in the bomber formation. Another bullet struck the windscreen diagonally forward and to the left, opening up a second hole the size of a fist. Then I felt like I was hit hard in my back.

'After releasing the bombs, the hentai commander's aircraft left the battlefield by diving and turning left at full speed. I was flying on the outside of the turning formation, so I gave the aircraft full throttle in an effort not to be left behind. I was worried about overheating the engines when one of the rear gunners hit my shoulder from behind and shouted, "The aeroplane's on fire!" "Where?" I replied. "Smoke is coming from under the engine", he answered. I told him, "Don't worry. Return to your station at once and shoot back at the enemy fighters". There was no fire. The fuel-air mixture ratio had changed when I opened the throttles, causing black smoke to pour out from the exhausts.

'About seven to eight minutes after we released the bombs, the enemy fighters stopped attacking and I was finally able to relax a little. The aerial battle lasted for 20 minutes, but it seemed to me that we had been fighting for an hour or two. After the enemy attack was over, we returned to cruising formation. During the battle, I couldn't afford to look at anything else because I had to concentrate on keeping the aeroplane in the formation. However, now that things had calmed down, I looked around and, to my surprise, I could only see the three bombers of our hentai. No 1st or 3rd Chutai and no escort fighters. I didn't know how we had managed to get ourselves separated or what had happened.

'Our three bombers from the 2nd Chutai were heading back to base when, about five minutes later, four fighters appeared behind us about 500 m above and to our left. It was almost dusk, and it was difficult to make out if they were friendly or not. After a while, they attacked us, and we changed to battle formation in a hurry. The enemy fighters turned around and attacked relentlessly, and our gunners did not respond. I felt hopeless. "What's wrong? Shoot back at once!", I shouted to our gunners, but only one or two of them started firing.

'Suddenly, I noticed that the outboard fuel tank of the starboard engine of the third bomber, flown by WO Kichisaburo Shimizu, had been hit and gasoline was trailing like a mist. It was close to the exhaust pipe, and I worried that it would catch fire, so I tried to send a message to the radio operator, Sgt Hiroshi Ito, telling him, "There is a risk the gasoline leaking from the right outboard tank will ignite. Cut down the fuel to the right engine!". When I failed to get through, I approached the bomber and tried to signal the crew. Shimizu, however, was anxiously looking at the starboard engine, and he didn't turn off the fuel. As a result, it ignited and the bomber exploded. Both wings and the tail broke up into half-a-dozen fireballs, before falling away into the sea south of Long Island. In the dimness of the sunset, lit by the spinning and burning aircraft, we joined hands to pray for our fallen comrades.

'Once back at base, I found out that our gunners had used up all their ammunition during the first air battle, and after closer inspection I counted 24 bullet holes in my bomber. My face was also cut in five places by

This Donryu has just had its port engine replaced by groundcrew working under the watchful eye of a chief engineer (standing with his back to the camera) (*Author's Collection*)

pieces of glass from the windscreen. An armour-piercing shell had hit the joint of my right thumb diagonally from the left front, peeling the skin off and leaving my glove soaked in blood. Another armour-piercing shell had struck near the centre of my back, but it had been stopped by the bulletproof steel plate that a member of our maintenance crew had installed just before taking off. The propellers, fuselage, centre wing section and tail were all hit, but no vital parts of the aircraft had received damage and all members of our crew safely returned to But.'

The 7th Sentai had in fact been attacked by 16 P-40N Warhawks of the 49th Fighter Group's 8th Fighter Squadron (FS), rather than 'Grummans' as stated by the Ki-49 crews. The destroyer USS *Reid* (DD-369), which was serving as an air picket ship, had spotted the IJAAF formation approaching the Allied warships. A fighter controller on board the destroyer had vectored the P-40Ns, which had been patrolling the area and were heading back to base, onto the Japanese aircraft. In the confusion of the battle that ensued, the Warhawk pilots identified the 'Helens' as IJNAF G4M 'Bettys', since both bomber types had tail turrets. USAAF pilot Lt Harold Sawyer reported;

'I just started for home when I saw a three-ship high to my right. I pulled up from a "two o'clock" position and saw they were "Betty" bombers. I fired a long burst at the lead ship, hitting its nose and right engine. Smoke came from the engine first, and then it started to burn. I then dragged my fire through the left wing of the bomber, rolled over and came home.'

Sawyer's account closely matches Okawa's narration of the plight that befell Shimizu's bomber, from the time and place of the encounter to the specific details of the starboard engine being hit and the damage done by the Warhawk's firing pass. Lt John Hanson claimed two 'Bettys' shot down and a third damaged (he was later credited with two victories). All in all, the 8th FS reported that ten Japanese aircraft had been shot down for the loss of the P-40 flown by Lt Roger Grant, whose aircraft was hit by cannon fire from one of the 'Helens', forcing him to bail out.

The IJAAF claimed that eight enemy fighters had been shot down, while recording the loss of one Ki-49, and noting that another had failed to return. A solitary fighter was also lost, a second failed to return and three were damaged. Bomber crews claimed that two 'cruisers' had been set on fire and a third had received a near miss. In actual fact, no Allied vessels were damaged. Two Ki-49s were sent out to attack enemy vessels that night.

On 22 September every available fighter was ordered to escort all serviceable IJAAF bombers in an all-out attack against the Allied fleet, even though heavy casualties were expected. At the same time, reports arrived that an IJN supply convoy was bound for Wewak that day. This prompted the HQ of the 7th Hikoshidan to ask the 4th Kokugun to clarify which mission was to take priority. It was duly told that the protection of the supply convoy was more important, so all fighters were to be placed in reserve in order to escort it.

Shortly after dawn on the 22nd, two Ki-46 'Dinahs' from the 10th Sentai (one from Rabaul and one from Wewak) and another from the 74th Independent Chutai patrolled the area. Their observations, in combination with reports from the IJA's 18th Army, finally provided the 4th Kokugun with a clear picture of the situation. The first wave of Allied troops had landed at Finschhafen, where anti-aircraft units were already operational covering the offloading of supplies.

The IJAAF responded with a series of raids, starting with six Ki-48s from the 45th Sentai that attacked the landing beach early in the morning at low-level. Next, two 'Helens' from the 61st Sentai attempted to repeat this feat in a high-altitude bombing run. However, it was rainy season and the weather was overcast, forcing crews to return to base without reaching their target. Further attacks were mounted by IJAAF and IJNAF bombers during the course of the morning.

By early afternoon, the 4th Kokugun realised the seriousness of the situation on the ground at Finschhafen and reversed its previous instructions prioritising the protection of the supply convoy over attacks on the Allied fleet. The 7th Hikoshidan was ordered to target the enemy vessels with all available aircraft. Nine 'Helens' (three from the 7th Sentai and six from the 61st Sentai), escorted by nine Ki-43s from the 24th Sentai and 12 from the 59th Sentai, as well as nine Ki-61s from the 68th and 78th Sentai, took off from Wewak airfield into a cloudless sky at around 1330 hrs. It took some time for all the units to gather overhead, and on the way to Finschhafen the weather rapidly deteriorated to the point where the bombers were forced to return home without dropping their ordnance, much to the disappointment of the 4th Kokugun and Lt Gen Teramoto.

Another attack on the Finschhafen landing area was attempted by the 7th Hikoshidan the following day, with seven 'Helens' being escorted by 27 fighters. Again, the weather was poor and the mission had to be abandoned.

Meanwhile, the much anticipated Wewak No 9 convoy, consisting of three transports (*Aden Maru*, *Taisei Maru* and *Yasukuni Maru*) and their escorts, entered the port of Wewak in the middle of the night of 23 September, and ammunition, fuel, food and supplies were quickly offloaded. The ships departed the following morning, and the IJAAF made every effort to protect the convoy. Unfortunately, the transports were intercepted by USAAF B-25s near Kairuru Island on the 26th and *Taisei Maru* was sunk.

The previous day, IJAAF bombers had been active over the Finschhafen landing area, with two Ki-21s from the 14th Sentai at Rabaul attacking at 0330 hrs, and two more following ten minutes later. Three 7th Sentai 'Helens' targeted a nearby airfield at 0435 hrs, and at 0600 hrs nine 'Lilys' escorted by 26 fighters bombed both the landing area and the airfield.

According to the official history of the 7th Sentai, this photograph was taken at But East airfield during 1943. Note the thatched huts under the palm trees behind the recently arrived Ki-49-II, the latter taxiing in with its Fowler flaps extended (*Author's Collection*)

During the early morning of 26 September, the 4th Kokugun attempted to coordinate an attack combining the forces of the 6th and 7th Hikoshidan. However, as a result of general miscommunication, at 0540 hrs just two Ki-49s from the 7th Sentai bombed an Allied heavy artillery position northwest of the Finschhafen landing area and troops near Heldsbach, before returning safely to base. Later in the day, an IJA unit in the area reported that one enemy heavy artillery piece had been completely destroyed and considerable casualties inflicted on Allied troops.

The following day, another attack was launched against Finschhafen, but six 'Helens' from the 7th and the 61st Sentai and their six escorting Ki-61s had to abort the mission due to bad weather. On 29 September two 61st Sentai 'Helens' succeeded in bombing Finschhafen during an early morning operation, after which the unit spent the rest of the day providing air cover for the departure of the Wewak No 10 convoy, which consisted of three transports (*Bengal Maru, Maya Maru* and *Yamagata Maru*) and their escorts – the vessels had arrived the previous night and immediately unloaded their supplies.

This convoy was the last of four to reach Wewak from mid-September, and the 'Helens' were particularly active providing escort for the vessels. Of the 12 transport ships in these convoys, ten arrived successfully. However, most of the provisions brought to Wewak were subsequently lost during intensive Allied air raids.

The end of September marked the departure of the 24th and 59th Sentai, which had escorted the 'Helens' on many of their recent missions. While both units relocated to the Philippines to recuperate and re-equip with new aircraft and pilots, the Donryu jubakutai were now reduced to a handful of serviceable bombers – the 7th Sentai had just nine on strength at But East, four or five of which were airworthy, while the 61st had six flyable Ki-49s at Wakde. Nevertheless, both units had to stay behind and continue to sporadically fly missions.

Following the successful Allied landing at Finschhafen and the failure of the IJA to counter-attack, the higher ground at Sattelberg, further inland, became the staging area from where subsequent Japanese attacks were planned. Due to the inaccessibility of the area, the supply of the units at Sattelberg fell to the Ki-49 sentai, whose aircraft flew a number of missions dropping packages by parachute from their bomb-bays. For three days from 23 October, two 'Helens' from the 7th Sentai and two from the 61st dropped much needed supplies in the Sattelberg area, despite the fact that these missions were flown either after sunset or before dawn, thus making the results difficult to confirm.

On 27 October, a major effort by the 7th Hikoshidan to supply troops in a risky daylight mission was organised involving nine 'Helens' from the 7th and 61st Sentai escorted by 25 fighters. Packages were dropped from

1530 hrs, and the bombers soon got into trouble. Kuninosuke Uchino was the flight engineer on board a 1st Chutai, 7th Sentai Ki-49 that participated in the mission. He recalled;

'As the weather improved, a formation of nine Donryu Model 2s, three from each chutai, was assigned to drop supplies to our troops. The sky above the drop zone was sunny, but above our formation, at an altitude of 3000 m, there were some cumulus clouds. When we received the signal, all the aeroplanes successfully dropped the provisions to the troops below. From the nine aeroplanes involved, 270 parachutes deployed like beautiful white flowers that bloomed in an instant, swaying and falling into the jungle. Some static lines were sticking out from the seams of the bomb-bays, blowing in the wind. I thought "Phew! This mission has gone smoothly".

'Suddenly, the 20 mm cannon in the rear turret began firing, followed by the 13 mm dorsal cannon and the nose-mounted machine gun. Curtiss P-40 enemy fighters had been loitering in the clouds above our formation, before attacking us all at once. I was the flight engineer, and was also assigned as a side gunner, and I ran to my mount and started shooting. There were about two-dozen enemy fighters, and they attacked from all directions. They were making quick passes from our rear, then turning around and attacking us again.

'After one of these passes, white smoke started pouring out from the forward fuselage of our aircraft. I hadn't previously noticed it because I was concentrating on manning my machine gun and shooting back. Sgt Maj Shigezaburo Fukui, a veteran turret gunner, had spotted it first and he then let me know. I stopped shooting and moved up to the cockpit. Our bomber had been hit in the outboard fuel tanks of the starboard wing, and flames were now shooting out. These were auxiliary tanks and didn't hold much fuel, so the fire would soon be extinguished.

'In the cockpit, Capt Mizoda, commander of the 1st Chutai, decided to leave the formation for a lower altitude. However, I urged him to "open the throttle lever and get back into formation". Mizoda calmly nodded and then tried to retake his place in the formation that was now heading back to base. Looking outside, I could only see six undamaged bombers, for the two on the left side of the formation were trailing black smoke and losing altitude.

'Soon after, the fire in the starboard wing of our aircraft went out, and I felt relieved for a moment. However, we had not yet reached our place in the formation, and the enemy fighters quickly picked us out for a series of relentless attacks. Soon, the starboard engine was hit and seized completely. Then the port engine seized. There was no fire, but both wings were full of bullet holes. One after the other, the enemy fighters attacked us, and I was wondering if any bullets would hit me. Fortunately, the fuselage was struck less times than the wings. We started to glide closer to the surface of the sea, and our primary pilot, WO Makoto Matsumoto (a classmate of mine), managed to smoothly operate the flaps and bring the aircraft to alight on the water. In retrospect, it's amazing that the flap system worked, even though our aircraft had received so many hits.

'The shock we received the moment the aircraft hit the water is indescribable. Nevertheless, it didn't sink immediately. I opened the canopy, climbed out and reached the wing, where I waited for everyone to come out. The nose gunner, Sgt Maj Shirai, (text continues on page 46)

COLOUR PLATES

1
Hamamatsu Rikugun Hiko Gakko (Hamamatsu Army
Flying School)

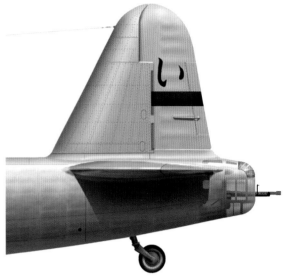

2
Rikugun Koku Seibi Gakko (Army Aircraft
Maintenance School)

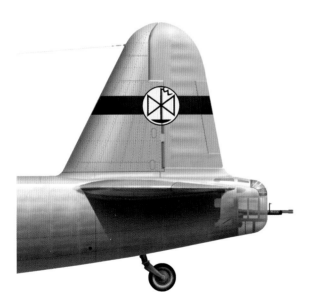

3
Rikugun Koku Tsushin Gakko (Army Flight Radio
Operators School)

4
11th Hikoshidan Shireibu Hikohan (11th Air Division
Headquarters Flight)

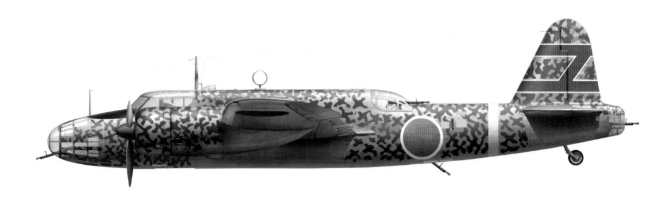

5
Ki-49 Model 2 Ko of the 61st Sentai,
2nd Chutai, Hollandia, New Guinea,
April 1944

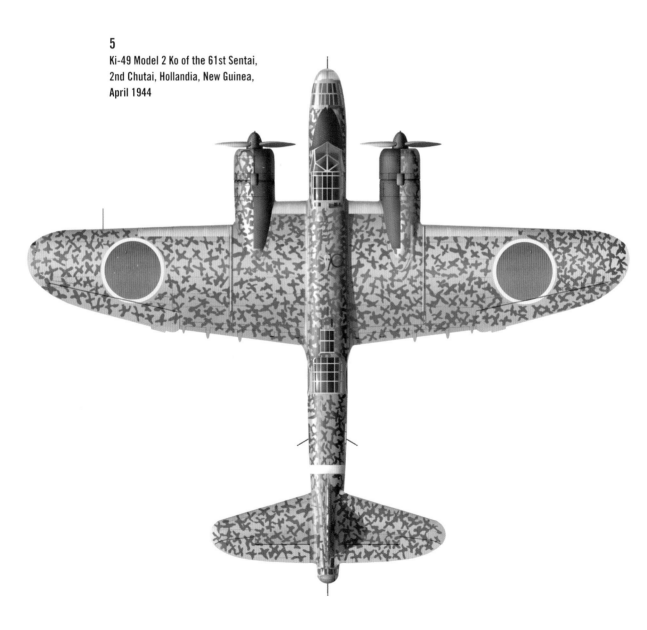

6

Hollandia, April 1944 (© *Jeffrey Ethell Collection*)

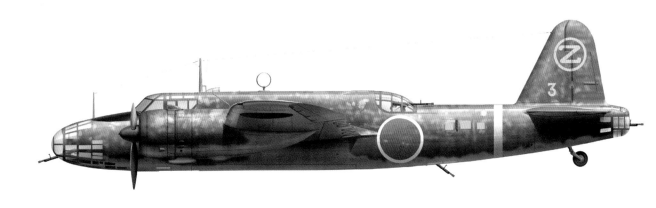

7
Ki-49 Model 2 Otsu of the 20th Independent
Chutai, Hollandia, April 1944

8
Wakde Island, May 1944 (© *Jeffrey Ethell Collection*)

9
Del Carmen airfield, the Philippines, 1945 (© *Jeffrey Ethell Collection*)

10 and 11
Del Carmen airfield, the Philippines, 1945 (© *Jeffrey Ethell Collection*)

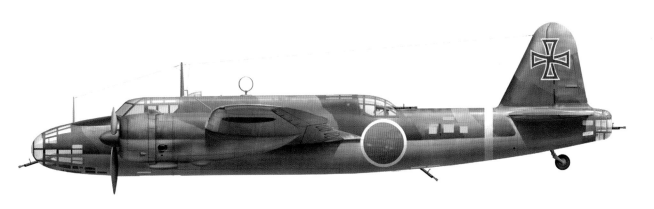

12
Ki-49 Model 2 Otsu of the 74th Sentai,
2nd Chutai, Del Carmen airfield,
the Philippines, 1944–45

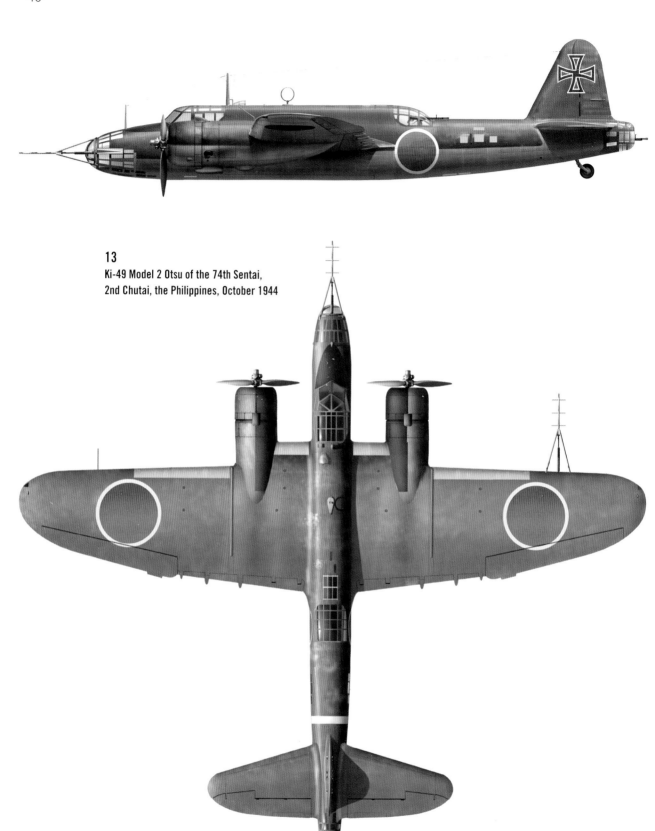

13
Ki-49 Model 2 Otsu of the 74th Sentai,
2nd Chutai, the Philippines, October 1944

14
Ki-49 Model 2 Otsu of an unknown unit, Nichols Field, the Philippines, 1945 (© *Jeffrey Ethell Collection*)

15
Ki-49 Model 2 Otsu of the 95th Sentai,
1st Chutai, Clark Field, the Philippines,
late 1944

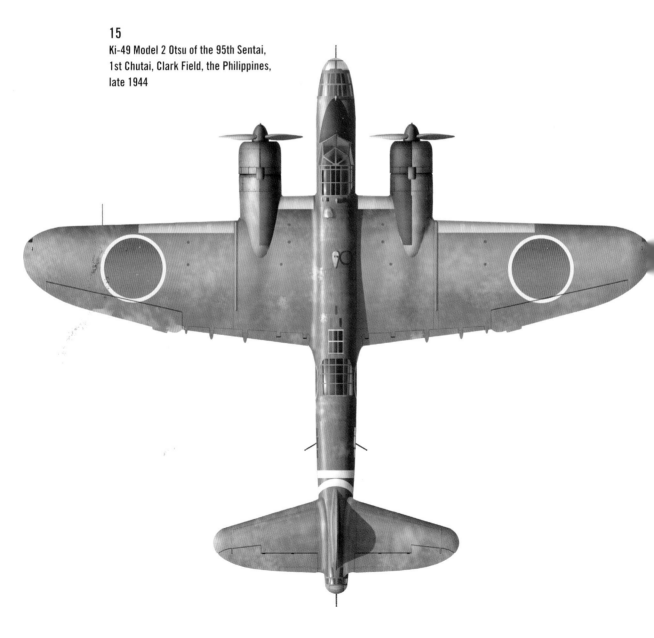

16
Ki-49 of an unknown unit, Nichols Field, the Philippines, 1945 (© *Jeffrey Ethell Collection*)

17
Ki-49s of an unknown unit, Yokota, Japan, 1945 (© *Jeffrey Ethell Collection*)

18
Ki-49 Model 2 Ko of the 62nd Sentai,
2nd Chutai, Hamamatsu, Japan, May 1943

19
Ki-49 Model 2 Otsu, Pitoe airfield, Morotai,
9 September 1945

was struggling to manoeuvre his way through the narrow passage to the cockpit. I started swimming without any difficulty because I was wearing a kapok life vest that kept me afloat. Unfortunately, our tail gunner, Sgt Maj Tomokichi Matsumoto, had been killed in action. Capt Mizoda threw his sword and pilot's boots into the sea and then removed Matsumoto's body from the tail of the sinking aeroplane. He held it beside him and swam to shore. There, we were helped by friendly infantry soldiers.

'A while later, we cremated Matsumoto's body, boarded a landing craft and reached Madang airfield. Once there, a Type 97 heavy bomber brought us back to But East airfield five days after we had taken off on that fateful mission.'

The Ki-49s had been attacked by eight P-40Ns of the 7th FS and nine P-39Ns of the 40th FS, which between them claimed to have shot down six Japanese bombers and seven fighters! The USAAF squadrons lost the P-39N flown by Lt William Owen in return.

November started with a reorganisation of the remaining IJAAF units in-theatre, and this included the transferring of the 7th and 61st Sentai to the 6th Hikoshidan. The first major raid mounted by the 6th took place on 23 November when five 'Helens' from the 61st and four from the 7th Sentai, escorted by 35 fighters, targeted Finschhafen yet again. 2Lt Yasuji Takata was the commander of the fifth aircraft in the 61st Sentai formation, and he recalled that each of the participating bombers was loaded with 15 50-kg bombs;

'[After successfully completing the bombing mission] our formation was leisurely flying in a northerly direction when, about an hour after we had passed Manus Island, one of the [Ki-49] gunners gave us the signal for an impending enemy attack by firing his cannon. An aircraft that looked like a fly in the distance was rushing through the clouds over the "Stanley" mountains on our left. We still couldn't tell if it was a friend or foe but cautiously assumed combat formation. Soon, we saw that it was a Lockheed P-38, ready to attack our left side from behind and above. The 20 mm cannons of all the bombers started shooting feverishly. The P-38 got closer, blasted a few bursts from beyond effective range and left.

'A few minutes later, a formation of three enemy fighter aircraft bravely approached and attacked at close range. My aeroplane received about a dozen hits, but the attack was soon over. Two of the three enemy fighters were on fire as they dived away, looking like they were going to crash. The third retreated by flying under our formation.

'Our aircraft was in the rear of the formation, and from what I could see all the other bombers were unharmed. I took a deep breath and noticed a strange smell in the cabin. It was different from the smell of gunpowder and it was like burning rubber and cloth. At first I thought the oxygen bottles had overheated, so I ordered the crew to throw them out. But the smell did not go away. Then I noticed a few bullet holes near the hinomaru on the port wing through which black smoke was starting to pour out.

'There was a high probability that incendiary ammunition had hit the cover of the gasoline tank. If left as it was, the gasoline tank could explode and there was no way to put out the fire. There were three possibilities – the ammunition had been stopped by the fuel cover, setting it on fire, or it had penetrated the cover and then been extinguished inside the fuel tank, or it had passed through the wing entirely. Fortunately, there was no fuel leaking from beneath the wing, so the last possibility was ruled out. The fuel tank was covered by layers of rubber, cloth and kapok some two centimetres in thickness. Once a bullet penetrated the tank, the rubber would seal the hole, preventing fuel from spilling out and catching fire.'

Takata tried to put out the fire by side-slipping, and in the process the bomber got separated from the rest of the formation. With the creeping fire still burning, he managed to land the Ki-49 at But East airfield. A groundcrewman who subsequently inspected the damage told Takata, 'If you look closely, there is still a hole in the fuel tank. It seems that the cover ignited before it was pierced by the incendiary bullet. Most of it is completely burned out. It's a miracle the fuel tank hasn't blown up'. It seems that the 'Helens' were attacked by a flight of four Lightnings that were probably from the 475th FG's 432nd FS at Nadzab. No casualties were reported during this encounter.

By late November the 7th Sentai had only four bombers in flyable condition and the 61st no more than five – the 59th Sentai, which had recently returned from the Philippines, could provide bomber escort with 13 Ki-43s. Both bomber units were also suffering a shortage of aircrew due to dysentery and malaria. The latter disease had hit the 7th Sentai particularly hard, killing both unit CO Maj Ohnishi Toyokichi and chutaicho Lt Toyokichi Endo during November. Nevertheless, on 1 December, 45 aircrew from the 7th were reassigned to the 61st as reinforcements, leaving the former with barely enough personnel to man its four operational 'Helens'.

On 12 December, after a long hiatus, the jubakutai of the 6th Hikoshidan managed to launch a raid against Nadzab airfield with nine Ki-49s. Although the weather was unfavourable, they succeeded in setting a number of Allied aircraft on fire – four reported by Japanese crews as being completely burned out, with many others damaged. However, three bombers were lost to defending fighters, including the aircraft flown by Lt Naoyoshi Kitamura of the 7th Sentai.

NEW BRITAIN

On 15 December the Allies launched Operation *Dexterity*, which included landings on the island of New Britain, off the northeast coast of New Guinea. Its aim was to secure the flank of the advance along the New Guinea coastline and reduce the effectiveness of the major Japanese base at Rabaul. On that date, at first light, US forces also landed on Arawe, located off the southwest coast of New Britain. This was a diversionary operation before the major amphibious assault at Cape Gloucester, on the northwestern coast of New Britain, on 26 December.

The Arawe assault succeeded in confusing the 4th Kokugun as to the primary aim of the Allied operation. Furthermore, early-morning sorties by IJAAF reconnaissance aircraft were hampered by heavy cloud over western New Britain. Some enemy activity was observed north of Finschhafen, however, with Australian troops advancing and eventually capturing Lakona as part of the Battle of Sio, a follow up to the Battle of Finschhafen.

Allied ships were also observed in the vicinity, and concluding that these were part of an invasion fleet, the 6th Hikoshidan sent out a force of six 'Helens' from the 7th and 61st Sentai escorted by 30 fighters at 1400 hrs. Mid-flight, crews received news from Rabaul informing them of the exact location of the enemy landing, and, as a result, the target of the bomber formation switched from Finschhafen to Arawe. After attacking the latter (and, according to Allied reports, inflicting only minimal damage), all the IJAAF aircraft involved safely returned to Hansa and Alexishafen airfields.

Another mission was mounted the following day when the weather had improved over western New Britain, with the same number of bombers being escorted by 34 fighters from the 59th and 248th Sentai. This time they encountered USAAF fighters and the operation ended in total disaster.

The group had gathered over Wewak at 1000 hrs and then climbed to an altitude of 4000 m near Umboi Island, between mainland New Guinea and New Britain. The aircraft were about to fly higher to 5500 m when they were ambushed by four P-38s. Soon after, 11 more Lightnings made a quick diving pass from the rear of the 248th Sentai. The 'Oscar' pilots tried to follow their opponents as they dived away, but the USAAF fighters had the advantage and easily outdistanced them. The 'dive-and-zoom' tactics of the American pilots could not be countered by the Ki-43s, and to make matters worse, there were cloud formations at 2000, 3000 and 6000 m. The bombers soon lost contact with their escorts as the 'Oscars' chased the P-38s in and out of the clouds.

While the bombers did manage to reach their target and release their bombloads, five of them and five fighters were shot down during the mission. The last surviving 'Helen' of the formation had to make an

This Model 2 'Helen' was found destroyed by US troops at Cape Gloucester. According to eyewitness reports, it had crash-landed here on 16 December 1943 – information that clearly indicates it was the only Ki-49 not immediately shot down during that day's ill-fated raid on the Allied invasion fleet off Arawe. The 7th Sentai's official history explains that that bomber belonged to this unit, and it was flown by 1Lt Motoo Neki. He and his crew survived the crash, after which they set their bomber on fire and then headed off to find friendly troops, which they duly did a few days later. This information confirms for the first time that the unit marking of the 7th Sentai was the two slanting lines just visible above the katakana 'I' on the fin. Other aircraft from the unit appear to have only one line visible, perhaps indicating a different chutai. Curiously, the unit never adopted a specific unit marking. 7th Sentai bombers have been erroneously recorded in the past as having an illustration of Mount Fuji as a tail marking. This was only occasionally applied when the unit was equipped with Ki-21s, and was never used when it operated Ki-49s (*Thomas A Laemlein Collection*)

emergency landing midway back to But East, although the crew was unharmed.

It seems the IJAAF formation had been very unlucky that day, for at about the same time the Japanese bombers were heading for their target (the landing area at Arawe), the 433rd FS/475th FG had been sent to escort V Bomber Command B-24 Liberators tasked with bombing Cape Gloucester. A flight from the unit had initially spotted the Japanese aircraft and engaged them, with a second flight from the 431st FS/475th FG then joining the melee. Following this one-sided action, the 433rd was credited with six kills and the 431st with three. The pilots involved incorrectly stated that they had downed 'Betty' bombers.

Ten days later, both IJAAF and IJNAF aircraft were committed in relatively large numbers in a series of attacks on the 1st Marine Division as it came ashore at Cape Gloucester. USAAF fighter pilots claimed 60+ Japanese aircraft destroyed on the 26th, and six Ki-49s from the 7th and 61st Sentai were amongst those lost. Shocked by such attrition, the 6th Hikoshidan ordered the stopping of all daylight raids. From then on, the few remaining Ki-49s would be employed exclusively at night, primarily on supply drop missions. Two Ki-49s from the 7th Sentai undertook the unit's final

This dramatic photograph was taken during the 3 February 1944 raid on But East airfield by B-25s from the 345th Bomber Group's 501st Bombardment Squadron. The Donryu in the foreground, which was probably a replacement aircraft as it lacks a tail marking, has already been set on fire by exploding ordnance. Behind it, more 23-lb AN-M40 Para-Frag bombs dropped by the Mitchells are about to hit the ground on either side of four Ki-61 'Tony' fighters (*NARA*)

For four consecutive days from 28 March 1944, USAAF B-24s mounted devastating raids on Hollandia airfield. On the 30th, three Ki-49s from the 61st Sentai that had relocated to the airfield earlier that day to participate in a raid on Allied positions were caught on the ground and destroyed, as can be seen in this photograph. Two aircrew (WO Ino and Sgt Akaishi) had gone to the maintenance area at the airfield to look for a replacement tailwheel for one of the bombers shortly after landing at Hollandia, and they were the only personnel from the 61st Sentai to survive the attack (*NARA*)

supply operation on 8 January 1944, resulting in the loss of Lt Ugakami.

The 7th had also been flying mail courier missions with five 'Helens' from late 1943, the aircraft performing regular flights between Ambob, Manila, Wakde, But East, Alexishafen, Wewak and Rabaul. These operations came to a halt on 17 January when the 7th Sentai was ordered to return to Hamamatsu for conversion onto the Mitsubishi Ki-67 'Peggy' bomber. The unit had lost 87 aircrew during its time in New Guinea.

IJAAF units had been powerless to prevent the Allied landings in northeast New Guinea and New Britain in the final months of 1943, and they were unable to stem the Allied advance along New Guinea's northern coast in early 1944. In Finschhafen, a new, greatly expanded airfield brought Allied fighters and bombers considerably closer to the major Japanese bases in Wewak and at But East. This in turn forced the IJAAF to relocate further to the rear in Western New Guinea, and only use But East as a forward airfield for quick refuelling and emergency landings.

This 61st Sentai Donryu was found destroyed at Hollandia following the 22 April 1944 landings. The fuselage windows indicate that the bomber was probably a Model 2 Ko, while its red tail markings denote the 'Helen's' assignment to the 2nd Chutai (*Joe Picarella Collection*)

The 61st Sentai had remained at Wakde throughout this period, and reinforcements in mid-January 1944 had briefly returned the unit to full strength with 15 serviceable Ki-49s. From here, the 61st conducted a series of small harassing raids with only one or two bombers against Allied bases, and it also flew regular transport and supply missions for the 4th Kokugun. Wakde was also far enough from Allied airfields to allow new aircraft to be received and replacement aircrew to be trained in relative safety. This did not remain the case for long, however.

A Ki-49 flown by Lt Kazuo Sakai was lost to USAAF P-38s on 3 March, this aircraft being one of the few 'Helens' downed in aerial combat during the period. Conversely, attacks by Allied bombers on Wakde had exacted a heavy toll, and by 13 March the 61st Sentai listed only five operational Ki-49s. Three days later, one of these aircraft was lost on take-off when WO Keizo Minami turned too sharply and stalled following an air raid warning.

March ended disastrously for the IJAAF. For four consecutive days from the 28th, and especially during the daylight attacks on the 30th and 31st, the airfield complex at Hollandia, on the north coast of Western New Guinea, was pummelled by a series of raids mounted by V Bomber Command B-24s. Hollandia was primarily an airfield depot where replacement aircraft arrived from Japan before they were allocated to combat units. In a repeat of the devastating Wewak raids of August 1943, 75 B-24s, escorted by almost 100 P-38s and P-47s, were able to deliver their ordnance totally unmolested. Any aircraft at Hollandia that survived

A second view of the 61st Sentai Ki-49 found abandoned at Hollandia airfield. The aircraft had almost certainly suffered damage in an Allied strafing attack on the base in the weeks prior to the invasion, the 'Helen' having been robbed of its engines, weaponry and flying surfaces for fitment to other Ki-49s in order to keep them operational (*NARA*)

the bombing were strafed by the fighters. Some Japanese sources state that close to 200 aircraft were destroyed during these raids.

With the Allied advance perilously close to Wakde by the end of March, the 61st was forced to relocate to Namlea airfield on Boeroe (present-day Buru) Island, in the Moluccas. Once the unit had settled in, from mid-April training of new crews commenced in earnest. Often paired with veteran crewmen, new pilots could clock up flying hours and gain much needed experience with the Ki-49 prior to being declared operational. As there were only a limited number of combat-ready 'Helen' bombers at Namlea, crews divided their time between flying convoy escort missions and anti-submarine patrols (see Chapter Four for details).

This heavily damaged Ki-49 was found by Allied troops at Awar airfield, near Hansa Bay, following the capture of the base in June 1944. Assigned to the 20th Independent Chutai for transport duties, the aircraft had the unit's numeral 2 inside a circle marking (symbolising the number 20) painted on its tail in yellow (*Australian War Memorial*)

CHAPTER THREE

BURMA

The 62nd Sentai was the only Ki-49-equipped unit to see action in Burma. Organised on 5 July 1939 at Hamamatsu and staffed by a handful of crews from the 7th Sentai, the 62nd initially consisted of just one chutai equipped with four Ki-21s. By September 1940 the unit had reached full strength with three chutai, each assigned nine Ki-21s. At the outbreak of the Pacific War, the 62nd was very active in the Philippines, where it bombed US military bases and airfields. For much of 1942 the unit flew from Mingaladon, in Burma, and the 62nd remained here until 28 May 1943 when it was transferred to Sungei Patani (present-day Sungai Petani) in the Malay Peninsula to rest and recuperate.

In January 1944 the 62nd returned to Japan, where it received brand new Ki-49s and replacement crews. A month was spent training and getting accustomed to the bombers under the leadership of new unit commander, and ex-infantry officer, Lt Col Nobumasa Haga.

To prepare for its reassignment back to Burma as part of the 5th Hikodan, the sentai spent two months at Sungei Patani. The airfield, located across from Penang Island, had been carved out of a rubber tree forest and it was in poor condition by early 1944. This contributed to a number of fatal accidents, and crews who preferred the 'Sally' complained that the 'Helens' engines and related systems were designed for the cold conditions of Manchuria and Siberia, not tropical climates.

A Ki-49 Model 2 Otsu of the 62nd Sentai takes off from Hamamatsu in early 1944 bound for Sengei Patani, in the Malay Peninsula. By early March the unit was at Hmawbi, in Burma (*Joe Picarella Collection*)

The Donryu was the first IJAAF bomber to feature a tail gun. The position was a rather crude design, resembling a bucket and a cage with an open rear end. In the early models of the Ki-49, a Te-4 machine gun was installed with nine spare magazines containing a total of 612 rounds (*Author's Collection*)

Nonetheless, on 5 March 1944 the unit reached its main base of Hmawbi, near Rangoon, just 24 hours before the start of Operation *U Go* – the IJA offensive against the British-held northeast Indian region of Manipur that culminated in the pivotal battles of Imphal and Kohima. The airfield had a reddish-brown runway and the barracks were in a neighbouring village built from bamboo and straw mats.

On 8 March the 62nd Sentai received orders to mount its first raid with the Ki-49 against Tinsukia airfield (known to the Allies as Dinjan) in Assam, India. The bombers, which were to be escorted by Ki-43s from the 204th Sentai, would initially fly to Shwebo airfield, in central Burma, which was the mid-way point to their target. Here, after being refuelled, the formation would rendezvous with more 'Oscars' from the 64th Sentai. This was a complex operation, and nothing went to plan.

That morning southern Burma was covered in fog, and the bombers' departure had to be postponed until the early afternoon. At 1230 hrs, all serviceable Ki-49s finally took off from Hmawbi together with the 'Oscars' from the 204th Sentai and two Ki-21 'pathfinders'. According to the plan, the 'Helens' were to land at Shwebo Central airfield and the 'Oscars' at Shwebo East airfield. Unfortunately, the bombers landed at Shwebo West airfield by mistake, where the 64th Sentai had relocated that same morning in preparation for the arrival of the Ki-49s. The airfield was used exclusively by fighters, leaving no room for the 'Helens'.

Following widespread confusion, the 62nd Sentai eventually took off again and moved to Shwebo Central airfield. It was already evening by the time all the crews had arrived, forcing the mission to be cancelled. The units were instructed to fly south to Meiktila airfield, and at 1700 hrs while getting ready for take-off, six P-51A fighters from the USAAF's 1st Air Commando Group made a surprise attack.

Although there were a handful of Ki-43s in the air on patrol, they were nowhere to be seen. With no time available to scramble additional fighters to protect the Shwebo airfields, five 'Helens' were set on fire and a sixth damaged. Those in flyable condition managed to reach Meiktila, where the crews of the destroyed bombers subsequently joined them after a challenging truck ride that had seen the transports strafed by Allied aircraft. The Ki-49s were misidentified as Ki-46s by the USAAF pilots, who also destroyed ten Ki-43s and damaged several more. To add to the 62nd Sentai's misery, the following morning one of the surviving bombers failed to gain altitude after taking off from Meiktila and crashed. Only two aircrew survived the subsequent inferno when the fuel-heavy bomber caught fire.

After the sentai returned to Hmawbi, it was heavily criticised by the HQ of the 5th Hikodan and other IJAAF units in-theatre for getting lost and landing at the wrong airfield. Soon after, the 62nd Sentai was split into day and night attack groups, operating 'Helens' and 'Sallys', respectively.

This Ki-49 Model 2 Otsu of the 105th Kyoiku Hiko Rentai is having its port engine maintained. Note the roughly applied camouflage on the previously natural metal uppersurfaces (*Author's Collection*)

The sentai finally saw action on 18 March when Ki-49s joined Ki-48s from the 8th Sentai and Ki-21s of the 12th Sentai (covered by Ki-43s from 64th and 204th Sentai) in an attack on Allied troops in the Indaw area. Broadway airfield was bombed and its radio and radar facilities totally destroyed. A fuel dump was also damaged.

On 27 March the 'Helens' got their chance to prove their worth. A total of nine bombers led by Lt Col Haga (who, having been severely reprimanded by his divisional commander following the 8 March debacle, was keen to clear his name) would be escorted by no fewer than 60 Ki-43s from the 50th, 64th and 204th Sentai. Their target was to be Ledo, which was the starting point of the 'Ledo Road' – a highway built during World War 2 as a supply route for men and materiel heading into China.

Again, the operation got off to a bad start when a Ki-46 sent north to reconnoitre the Ledo area and check on weather conditions suffered radio failure, preventing the crew from informing the 62nd Sentai that the target was covered in thick cloud. The nine bombers and their escorts duly took off lacking this crucial information, forming up without any mishaps and eventually reaching the target area. That is where the trouble began. Sgt Koichi Naganuma was a dorsal gunner in one of the 'Helens' that participated in the mission, and he described what happened over Ledo;

'At that time, the rainy season was approaching in northern Burma, the Arakan Mountains were covered with clouds and there were middle-altitude clouds along our route. We were at an altitude of 7000m, and on our right we could see the Himalayan mountain tops peeking above the clouds.

'Around 1200 hrs, a friendly fighter spotted an enemy aeroplane, and the escort fighters flying on our side responded, but without success. At 1225 hrs we arrived over the target. Although we began the bombing run led by our commander's aircraft, the route was blocked by the clouds and we could not see the target, so the formation lowered its altitude to get under the clouds. It was at that point two P-51 fighters attacked the 2nd hentai from behind, about 50 m below us. There was an immediate reaction to this attack, with the commander of the 2nd hentai lowering his altitude still further while trailing white smoke. Then the second and third aircraft of the 2nd hentai disappeared from sight.

'P-51s appeared one after another, and a fierce aerial battle with our Hayabusa fighters began. My formation was also fighting feverishly with the enemy aircraft when suddenly the sentai commander's bomber disintegrated in mid-flight. At the same time, the second and third aircraft of the 1st hentai were ablaze, and they also started losing altitude. By then, only the 3rd hentai was still unharmed. While fighting off enemy aircraft on the left and right, my aeroplane was attacked from above and below at the same time. Two crewmen, Sgts Nakamura and Ujiie, were killed and I also suffered wounds to my face and back. The cannon mount I was manning was badly damaged and fell into the cabin. I placed a glove on my facial injury and tied it up with a bandage. I took a look at our tail gunner, Sgt Miura, but he wasn't moving at all.

'I grabbed the side gun to pull myself up and saw that there were countless holes in the fuselage and wings. The aircraft had lost considerable altitude, and I could now see the surrounding mountains from up close. The enemy aeroplanes were nowhere to be seen. When I looked up, there was nothing but the clear blue sky, and I wondered where that fierce aerial battle had gone.

'Moments later I spotted two P-38 Lightnings making an attacking run on us from behind, but their bullets passed in front of our aircraft. Looking down, I could see an enemy airfield. Two aircraft were taking off from the runway, so we dropped our Ta-Dan bombs. The pilot then turned for home, and initially no enemy aircraft chased after us. However, after a while, a small aircraft was spotted approaching from behind once again. As it got closer, I noticed that it was a Hayabusa fighter. The aircraft flew off to one side as our escort for a brief period before the pilot eventually rocked his wings in farewell and then dived away to the left. We were now alone.

'When we crossed the Arakan Mountains, the engine note suddenly changed. I was in a semi-unconscious state due to the pain of my injuries by then, and I only came back to my senses when we crash-landed. When I got out of the aeroplane and looked around, we were in the middle of the countryside. I saw white smoke rising from an engine that had fallen off and 1Lt Ohno, Sgt Taniguchi and Cpl Okibayashi standing beside the aircraft.

'After a while a Burmese policeman arrived, picked me up and put me in an ox cart. Then, the bodies of Nakamura, Ujiie and Miura were wrapped in a parachute and placed in the cart too. All the survivors reached a field hospital in Sagaing [located on the banks of the Irrawaddy River, 20 km to the southwest of Mandalay], and I was soon sent back to Japan to have my wounds treated. It was then that I lost contact with the rest of the crew.'

The 62nd Sentai had had eight bombers shot down during the course of the Ledo mission, and the last one (with Naganuma aboard as a gunner) crash-landed and was written off. The escorting 64th Sentai lost two aircraft and the 204th one. The formation had been attacked by P-51A and A-36As from the 311th Fighter-Bomber Group and P-40N Warhawks from the 89th and 90th FSs of the 80th FG and the 20th Tactical Reconnaissance Squadron. The USAAF in turn lost two P-51As and a P-40N. The day attack group of the 62nd Sentai had been devastated, losing all of its aircraft, the experienced chutai commanders and its sentai commander, Lt Col Haga (who was flying his first combat mission with the unit).

Despite the heavy attrition, the 62nd continued to undertake night attacks whenever possible. On 3 April two Ki-49s were lost whilst targeting Imphal, the bombers being intercepted by radar-equipped RAF Beaufighters of No 176 Sqn. Having lost a handful of aircraft on night operations since late March, the 62nd Sentai relocated to Sungei Patani on 29 May, where it was joined by reinforcements and a new sentai commander, the very experienced Lt Col Terushi Ishibashi (who had served as chutai commander with the Ki-21-equipped 60th and 98th Sentai). Post-war, he recalled;

'When I was assigned as commander of the 62nd Sentai I knew nothing about the unit, and was ordered to go to Hamamatsu with Capts Watanabe and Ito and about 50 aircrew. We were assigned ten Donryu bombers from the Utsunomiya aviation arsenal and received orders to relocate to Burma as reinforcements. It was only then that I found out about the grave losses the sentai had suffered during the Ledo attack. Although I was saddened by the death of the former sentai commander, Lt Col Haga, I decided that I should not follow his approach to leadership. Instead, I would calmly and carefully study the details and progress of each mission.

'After joining the unit, I did not give any rousing speeches. I paid attention to the maintenance of the bombers, and demanded that the groundcrews should do everything possible to improve performance. The Donryu's engines were prone to failures when they were running at full power.

'While at Sungei Patani, each chutai commander focused on bringing the unit back up to optimum combat strength. The training was intense and my encouragement was not necessary since everybody was determined and knew what they had to do. After the end of basic training, a minimum of two years is needed in order for the crews to become proficient in day and night missions, even for the most skilled crews. Losing highly proficient pilots due to engine malfunctions during take-off was particularly painful for me. I was torn between asking for more intensive training or cutting back on such flying in order to reduce the accident rate. Damn the Donryu bomber with its unreliable engines!

'Originally, the aircraft had been designed so that it eradicated the shortcomings of the Type 97 heavy bomber, but it took considerable effort to keep a Donryu serviceable, as parts had to be replaced all the time. The differences between the two bomber types were substantial. Because of the Donryu's unreliable engines, accidents often occurred whenever maximum power was required, such as during take-off. The maximum speed was also limited to 400 km/h. Later, when I was attacked by P-38s during a Morotai raid, and succeeded in evading them by running the engines at full speed, reaching 420km/h at a height of 8000 m, I cannot help but think that it was only through the grace of God that I escaped from the jaws of death.'

The 62nd never returned to the Burma front, for on 22 August the 4th Kokugun's 2nd Hikoshidan (to which the unit had been reassigned upon its withdrawal to Sungei Patani from Hmawbi) relocated to Api, in northern Borneo.

In the official history of the 62nd Sentai, Lt Col Terushi Ishibashi, commander of the unit, explains that the Donryu 'was originally designed to improve the shortcomings of the Type 97 heavy bomber ["Sally"], but it took a long time to maintain, and parts had to be constantly replaced'. There is no doubt that from a logistics standpoint, the IJAAF's decision to send Ki-49s to Burma rather than additional Ki-21s (examples of which had been in-theatre since 1942) significantly increased the maintenance burden of already overworked groundcrew (*Author's Collection*)

CHAPTER FOUR

OVER WATER, WESTERN NEW GUINEA AND MOROTAI

A Ki-49 Model 1 of the Hamamatsu bombing school has its engines run up prior to taking off on another night training flight. During the air campaign following the Allied landings on Morotai on 15 September 1944, IJAAF bombers mounted a series of particularly successful night missions that were only effectively opposed by anti-aircraft fire – the latter claimed all the 'Helens' lost by the 62nd Sentai during these sorties. Allied nightfighters, although available, found it virtually impossible to engage the Japanese bombers because mountains to the north of Morotai airfield prevented ground radar from detecting IJAAF Ki-21s and Ki-49s in time for aircraft to be scrambled to intercept them (*Author's Collection*)

Usually, IJAAF units would not fly over water, as for many years they had been preparing themselves for a future confrontation with the USSR, leaving everything sea-related to the IJNAF. From mid-1942, however, when jubakutai units were assigned to Southeast Asia to free up the IJNAF to concentrate on the campaign in the Solomon Islands, they were inevitably allocated anti-submarine and maritime patrol missions. Although units gradually became more confident flying over the Indian and Pacific Oceans, their crews lacked sufficient training to undertake the anti-submarine missions and their aircraft were not equipped for such a role. To make matters worse, there was little in the way of cooperation with IJNAF units.

As noted in Chapter Two, the 61st Sentai had retreated from Wakde to Namlea at the end of March 1944, from where its handful of crews flew ship escort, maritime patrol and anti-submarine missions. Convoys from Japan brought supplies and troops to the port of Wasile on Halmahera Island, and the unit often sent aircraft to Galela airfield, also on Halmahera, to provide air cover for these vessels.

Pilot 2Lt Yasuji Takata of the 61st Sentai's 3rd Chutai was assigned an anti-submarine patrol mission on 22 April 1944, taking off from

Galela airfield along with several other Ki-49s in order to maximise the coverage offered by the unit. The IJN had notified the 61st that there were no friendly submarines in the area, which meant that if Ki-49 crews spotted one it was safe to assume it was an enemy vessel and they were clear to attack it. Takata gave the following account of the mission in his memoirs;

'Immediately after take-off, I followed the prearranged flight route and proceeded in a straight line at an altitude of 1500 m as planned. All I could see from the cockpit was small waves breaking white and nothing else. It's boring to just stare at the surface of the sea, so after about an hour, I took control of the aeroplane and let Sgt Hayashi [the main pilot of the bomber] rest. About 30 minutes later I changed course, confirming our current position on the map in relation to our base. It was at this point I was convinced that we were going to return home empty handed.

'While flying about 600 km from Galela I spotted something that resembled a ship slightly to the left of our flightpath. Upon closer inspection, it appeared to be a submarine. I immediately told Sgt Hayashi and the rest of the crew to get ready to attack. I thought it was a submarine, but I had to make sure it wasn't one of our own ships or a fishing boat. However, from that distance it was too small to be sure. Our aeroplane was now flying lower and lower, and we could clearly see that it was a submarine heading west towards Mindanao Island, in the Philippines.

'I levelled the aeroplane off and pretended to overfly it, trying to convince the crew of the submarine that they hadn't been spotted. We had been trained to fly some ten kilometres away from an enemy submarine at an altitude of about 700 m, before suddenly reversing our course and attacking it from behind. When we passed down the left side of the submarine, it suddenly started diving, dropping its bow beneath the surface of the water. At that moment I decided to attack immediately, ordering Hayashi to dive at the submarine. Meanwhile, I opened the bomb-bay doors, grabbed the bomb release key and got ready to attack without using a bombsight. As the submarine's bow was thrust below the surface of the sea, its stern protruded above the water – the vessel resembled a duck diving for food.

'I was very surprised to see this sudden dive, as I knew very little about submarines and the way they operated. I thought that they would only move up and down horizontally when diving or surfacing. When little more than 100 m from the target, I dropped one 50-kg bomb by intuition and experience. It fell so fast I wasn't sure if I had hit the target. I saved the other bomb in case we had to make a second pass. When the bomber levelled out, we could see debris and oil all over the surface of the sea. I told Hayashi and the other crew members, "These floating objects are certainly from the submarine. The bomb hit it!", and decided to make another pass to confirm.

'However, in our excitement, both Hayashi and I couldn't find exactly where we had attacked the submarine because I had forgotten to check the compass prior to dropping the bomb. We kept looking for the submarine at different altitudes and, at some point, while we were flying close to the surface, I spotted more oil, pieces of wood, cans and half-a-dozen pieces of cloth. But no submarine. Thinking that our target had received a direct hit and been sunk, I sent messages back to sentai headquarters and Galela. We then headed home, feeling proud of what we had achieved.'

Releasing small quantities of oil, garbage and other waste via torpedo tubes was a classic technique used by submarine crews to fool their surface attackers into believing that they had been hit and sunk. Takata's attack showcases the little experience IJAAF crews had in anti-submarine warfare, and the complete lack of any technological assistance that could help them be more successful in carrying out this vitally important mission.

WAKDE – BIAK – NOEMFOOR

As part of the campaign to wrestle Western New Guinea from the control of the Japanese, and as a first step in preparation for the planned invasion of the Philippines, Allied forces captured the islands of Wakde (Battle of Wakde – Operation *Straight Line* – from 17–21 May 1944), which had formerly been home to the 61st Sentai, Biak (Battle of Biak, from 27 May to 17 August 1944) and Noemfoor (Battle of Noemfoor, from 2 July to 31 August 1944).

The units of the 4th Kokugun, which had evacuated its headquarters from New Guinea, were largely depleted of aircraft and crews and could

This Donryu bombardier is operating a Type 88 Model 3 bombsight, located behind the nose gunner. In the co-pilot's position there was either a Type 99 Light Reflector bombsight or a Model 2 Vector bombsight (*Author's Collection*)

not effectively launch attacks against Allied forces during any of these campaigns. Only night raids by a very limited number of aircraft (including just four serviceable Ki-49s of the 61st Sentai on 25 May 1944) could be organised, and the bombers would have to make refuelling stops at airfields halfway between Namlea and their assigned targets. To make matters worse, the weather in the area during the spring and summer of 1944 was mostly unfavourable, seriously restricting air operations.

The first mission undertaken by the 61st Sentai over Western New Guinea took place during the night of 26 May, when two 'Helens' under the overall command of Capt Sakurai bombed Wakde airfield. Allied groundcrews had been working on aircraft at the site under floodlights, and the latter allowed the Ki-49s to drop their ordnance with great accuracy. Releasing their bombs from an altitude of 4000 m, both crews claimed to have damaged 20 aircraft on the ground. Airfield facilities were also hit. Although Sakurai's bomber was damaged by anti-aircraft fire, it made it back to Namlea.

The following night, a solitary 'Helen' targeted Wakde once again, and its ordnance started a huge fire. The bomber was intercepted by enemy nightfighters whilst

heading home, but it also returned to base without having suffered any significant damage. Shortly after dawn that same day (27 May), US forces landed on Biak Island. Over the following days the troops were harassed by Ki-43 and Kawasaki Ki-45 'Nick' fighters, as well as Ki-48s and Mitsubishi Ki-51 'Sonia' ground attack aircraft.

When the IJA on Biak prevented US forces from capturing the island's airfield, the latter seized neighbouring Owi Island on 2 June and, within the space of a week, built an airfield on it comprising two two-kilometre-long runways.

On 5 June the 61st Sentai launched a multi-target night attack with all four of its operational bombers. Two 'Helens' were to bomb Wakde airfield, one was to attack Bosnek (the main landing beach for US forces on Biak) and the last one was to target the new airfield on Owi Island. A few hours earlier, two G4M 'Betty' bombers from the 732nd Kokutai and one from the 753rd Kokutai were scheduled to fly a mission against Wakde. One of them got lost and instead bombed the alternative target, Bosnek beach, at midnight. The remaining two had successfully targeted Wakde airfield 30 minutes earlier. They were followed by the two 'Helens', which released their bombs against Wakde at 0115 hrs, while the single bombers hit Owi at 0125 hrs and Bosnek beach at 0240 hrs. All the 'Helens' returned to base unharmed, despite having encountered heavy anti-aircraft fire over Wakde.

The following morning (6 June), an IJAAF reconnaissance aircraft reported that about 100 enemy aircraft could be seen on Wakde airfield, and 70 of them had been seriously damaged during the raids of the previous night. In their haste to repair damaged facilities at Wakde following the capture of the airfield, USAAF engineers had had insufficient time to build dispersed fuel and ordnance dumps and revetments for the aircraft, leaving the latter parked dangerously close to each other. Official US sources note that five men were killed and four wounded during the attack on Wakde, whilst six aircraft were destroyed and 80 damaged. Official Japanese reports at the time credit the surprisingly successful mission to both the IJAAF and IJNAF bombers that participated in the two raids.

During missions (this one being a night training flight by a Hamamatsu Ki-49 and crew under instruction) involving a number of bombers flying in formation, strict radio silence was observed and the formation commander's bomber communicated with the rest of the aircraft using the flight signal system. A yellow signal meant 'prepare to bomb (open bomb-bay doors)', a blue signal signified 'prepare the bomb release key', and, finally, when the commander put up the red signal, this instructed the rest of the bombardiers to 'simultaneously release their bombload' (*Author's Collection*)

For the next seven weeks the units of the 4th Kokugun rebuilt their strength, with the 61st Sentai also carrying out escort missions for supply ships in the area. Finally, in early August, the 61st commenced flying night raids once again. The first missions were hampered by bad weather, but on the 8th Capt Sakurai successfully bombed Namber airfield, on Noemphor Island, and one of his gunners claimed to have shot down an enemy nightfighter that attempted to intercept the Ki-49. Six days later, two more 'Helens' encountered Allied nightfighters while taking off from Langgur airfield, on Kai Island, on a mission against Biak and they were both lost.

In the wake of this unsuccessful operation, the unit's 'Helens' flew convoy escort duties until 25 August, when a single bomber undertook an evening mission against the airfield recently built for Allied fighters on Middleburg Island, one of the two Mios Soe (present-day Mios Su) Islands. The Ki-49 released its bombload at 1955 hrs, having encountered both heavy anti-aircraft fire and an enemy nightfighter during the course of the mission. Nevertheless, the 'Helen' managed to return to base unharmed.

A few days later several aircraft from the 61st Sentai relocated to Ambesia airfield on Celebes (present-day Sulawesi) Island, while most of the unit stayed put in Namlea.

On 1 September, Capt Suzuki and his crew targeted Biak Island's Sorido airfield, and although he radioed back to Namlea that he had successfully completed the mission, the Ki-49 failed to return to base. Nine days later, during the evening of 10 September, 2Lt Numata flew a mission against Middleburg Island. The bomber was intercepted by USAAF fighters, which knocked out one engine. In an effort to make it back in the crippled Ki-49, the crew threw out all the machine guns, ammunition and everything else that was not deemed vital to the aircraft's survival. Miraculously, the pilot managed to belly land at Bula airfield on Ceram Island in the Moluccas. The bomber had covered a distance of more than 360 km on one engine.

Bula airfield was under constant attack by enemy aircraft, and since they could not get their bomber repaired, the crew had to follow the shoreline on foot all the way to Amahai airfield on the south coast of the island – a distance of no less than 400 km. They finally returned to the 61st Sentai in October.

MOROTAI

On the morning of 15 September 1944, Allied forces landed on the strategically important island of Morotai (Battle of Morotai, from 15 September to 4 October), in the Moluccas. The island had been identified by the Allies as the perfect location for an airfield from which fighters and bombers could support operations in the Philippines, the liberation of which was planned for later that year.

Once it had received word of the invasion, the IJAAF's 7th Hikoshiden sent orders to the 61st Sentai instructing it to immediately commence a series of urgent single-aircraft night attacks with its force of five serviceable 'Helens'. The next evening (16 September), 2Lt Ichiro Miyake and his crew were the first to be sent into action from Ambesia on what they were soberly informed would be a one-way mission – the first of its kind for the 61st. Miyake's orders were clear. He was to bomb the enemy ships and then ram them with his aircraft, which lacked sufficient fuel for the return flight to Namlea. The 61st's aircrew were left in a state of shock following the receipt of this order.

Two hours after take-off, Miyake had reached the west coast of Halmahera when new orders arrived from the headquarters of the 7th Hikoshiden. The 61st Sentai was to relocate to Java Island and exchange its 'Helens' for brand new Ki-67 'Peggy' bombers. Immediately, the commander of the 61st radioed Miyake to abort the mission and return to base. Fortunately, the message was received, but having by then used most of his fuel, Miyake had to land at the IJNAF airfield at Menado (present-day Manado, on Sulawesi Island), refill his tanks and then return to Ambesia the following day.

A B-24 Liberator of the RAAF on a leaflet-dropping mission targeting IJA positions in Borneo on 11 June 1945 flies over the wrecked remains of 62nd Sentai, 3rd Chutai Ki-49 Model 2 serial number 3484 in the Brunei Bay area of Labuan (*Australian War Memorial*)

As ordered, the 61st relocated to Malang airfield on Java Island, and on 5 October it set off for Japan. The first stop was Labuan airfield on the north coast of Borneo, followed by Clark Field in the Philippines. While there, the crews said goodbye to their 'Helens' and were then flown home aboard transport aircraft.

Now it was the turn of the 62nd Sentai to attack Allied forces on Morotai. On 6 October six Ki-49s from the unit relocated first to Pinrang airfield on Celebes Island, before reaching Namlea the following day. At midnight on 8 October two 'Helens' flew a night raid against Morotai, reporting good results, although the bomber of Capt Oshita failed to return to base. The raid was repeated the next night with two more aircraft, but a third attempt on the 11th had to be aborted due to unfavourable weather conditions. The remaining 'Helens' were then pulled back to Pinrang before flying on to Sungei Patani, where crews recuperated and the surviving aircraft were serviced at the conclusion of this first phase of operations over Morotai. On 19 October the unit was transferred to San Jose airfield on Mindoro Island, in the Philippines, where it received an additional nine 'Helens'. This allowed the 62nd to form three fully equipped chutai.

Meanwhile, on Morotai, US Army and RAAF engineers had completed two airstrips with three large runways and hardstandings for 253 aircraft, including no fewer than 174 heavy bombers (which quickly commenced raids against targets in the Philippines), on the southern coast of the island by November.

The 4th Kokugun reacted by placing the 7th Hikodan, which included three jubakutai (the 12th and the 14th Sentai equipped with 'Sallys' and the 62nd Sentai) under the control of the 7th Hikoshiden, with orders for the aircraft to launch repeated attacks against Morotai. However, the presence of so many Allied day fighters over the island meant that the IJAAF bombers could mount nothing more than harassing night attacks, with very limited results. Furthermore, as in the first phase of operations

Another photograph of Ki-49 Model 2 serial number 3484. From this angle, its fuselage windows for the waist gunner suggest that, more specifically, it was a Model 2 Otsu. Huge bomb craters filled with water were a problem for RAAF engineers tasked with making captured Japanese airfields operable for Allied aircraft. Here, they are taking a survey of the water depth in a bomb crater to determine the level of drainage necessary (*Australian War Memorial*)

flown by the 61st Sentai in-theatre, the Ki-49s had to be based on airfields on Celebes Island – as far as possible from the increasing reach of Allied aircraft – and make stopovers at Namlea or airfields on Halmahera Island when targeting Morotai.

On 5 November four Ki-49s of the 62nd Sentai relocated to Kendari airfield on the southeastern corner of Celebes Island. The first raid by two bombers on Morotai scheduled for the following night had to be called off after Allied aircraft targeted Namlea airfield. Another attempt on the night of the 7th was aborted when the two bombers involved encountered unfavourable weather.

On 9 November the unit changed its target when a number of aircraft were sent to bomb Sansapor on the northern coast of Western New Guinea. The Ki-49s initially relocated to Liang on Ambon Island, in the Moluccas, but a heavy squall turned the unpaved runway at the airfield into a veritable 'sea of mud', rendering it unusable. The next night, a solitary 'Helen' managed to reach Namlea airfield and launch a night raid against Morotai, its crew subsequently claiming to have set a number of installations on fire. On 12 November the unit withdrew to Malang in order to perform essential maintenance on its aircraft, before flying a final raid on Morotai with two Ki-49s on the night of the 15th.

Although the 62nd Sentai would not undertake any more missions to Morotai, the two Ki-21-equipped jubakutai continued to attack Allied forces on the island. They were particularly successful on 22 November, when ten 'Sallys' from the 12th and the 14th Sentai bombed Morotai airfield, destroying eight bombers and damaging 28. The 7th Hikoshiden would repeatedly target the island airfield for several months, generating 172 sorties – 45 (33 by heavy bomber and 12 by fighter units) were deemed to have been successful – from the beginning of November 1944 until 10 January 1945. Some 42 Allied aircraft were destroyed and 33 damaged, with 19 servicemen killed and 99 wounded.

CHAPTER FIVE

THE PHILIPPINES

On 20 October 1944, US forces launched the anticipated amphibious assault on the island of Leyte, in the Philippines, landing in Tacloban and the neighbouring town of Dulag (Battle of Leyte, from 20 October to 31 December 1944). The 4th Kokugun based in Manila under the command of Lt Gen Kyoji Tominaga had made preparations to counter this offensive in a detailed plan called Operation *Sho-1*. It saw the movement of IJAAF units to newly constructed airfields in North Borneo and in the Philippines.

Just 24 hours prior to the invasion, the 62nd Sentai had arrived at San Jose airfield in order to receive additional Ki-49s to make good recent attrition. The unit, which at the time was based at Jesselton airfield (known to the Japanese as Api – the present-day Kota Kinabalu airport) on the northwest coast of Borneo, facing the South China Sea, was under the command of the 7th Hikodan, 2nd Hikoshidan. The 62nd Sentai was immediately ordered to relocate from San Jose to Manapla airfield (known as Carolina airfield to the Allies) on Negros Island, in the Philippines, from where it was to participate in retaliatory attacks on the invasion force.

The bombers newly issued to the unit at San Jose were in poor condition, but following hard work by maintenance crews ten 'Helens' were despatched to Manapla on 20 October. Soon after the 62nd had arrived there, it was ordered to mount an attack on US Navy vessels supporting the Leyte landings. Six 'Helens' led by Capt Watanabe took to the air at

A very rare photograph of a 95th Sentai Donryu at Zhendong airfield in Manchuria. The Model 1 was delivered from the Nakajima factory in the typical camouflage scheme for Ki-49s based in Manchuria – green, mustard yellow and brown for the uppersurfaces and grey for the undersides. The white slanting band on the fuselage indicates that the aircraft was flown by the 1st Chutai of the unit. Its propeller spinners were also painted in the same colour (*Author's Collection*)

1720 hrs and, once over Leyte, they were 'greeted' by an unprecedented hail of anti-aircraft fire. A veteran pilot who survived the mission described that it was like flying through 'a squall in reverse'. Despite the loss of two Ki-49s, the commander of the 7th Hikodan, Col Hiroshi Akira, ordered the 62nd to undertake a second attack with six more bombers in the early hours of the following day (21st).

That night, heavy torrential rainfall left the unpaved runway at Manapla muddy and soft. No bombers could take off as their wheels quickly became buried, whilst those that did manage to free themselves skidded on the slippery ground. In the end, despite these difficulties, three 'Helens' got airborne, only for the bomber of Sgt Maj Mano of the 1st Chutai to crash and burst into flames moments after take-off. The remaining two Ki-49s headed to Leyte, where they were almost certainly shot down – neither returned to Manapla. One of the 'Helens' was flown by 1Lt Ono, who had survived the ill-fated attack on Ledo on 27 March 1944.

In just two days the sentai had lost five of its precious 'Helens', with only the aircraft of unit commander Maj Ishibashi having completed these early missions unscathed. On 22 October Ishibashi loaded all surviving aircrew aboard his bomber and flew back to Jesselton. Early the following morning, a telegram from Col Akira arrived with orders for the 62nd to relocate immediately to Clark Field, on Luzon, from where it was to participate in a major attack scheduled for the 24th. Ishibashi protested that the unit had just been pulled out of the frontline, and that one more day was needed for maintenance of its surviving Ki-49s. He received the following terse response from the 4th Kokugun HQ;

'What's the meaning of this delay to deploy when the fate of the nation is in peril?'

Nevertheless, Ishibashi stubbornly insisted that one more day was necessary if the 62nd was going to support operations with all eight aircraft then at Jesselton. Finally, during the afternoon of 24 October, the unit flew to Clark Field.

The results of a large-scale attack on the 23rd had had a disastrous effect on all the IJAAF bomber units that had participated, with some having lost all of their aircraft. It was probably the high casualty rate and inefficiency of these early missions that forced the 4th Kokugun to revise its future plans for attacks on Leyte, sparing the 62nd from total annihilation. Daylight raids were abandoned and new orders issued that stipulated all aircraft capable of operating at night should use the cover of darkness when mounting attacks on airfields that had fallen into enemy hands.

Even so, nocturnal operations required thoroughly trained and very experienced crews, and only two pilots, Capt Hidaka and WO Nakajima, had the necessary expertise in the 62nd. Ishibashi prudently chose to send them on single-aircraft missions against Dulag and Tacloban airfields until 2 November, without losing any bombers. From then on, the sentai was ordered to resume its attacks on Morotai (as detailed in the previous chapter), and by the end of the month its remnants were at Malang airfield in East Java.

Out of the blue new orders arrived, sending the unit back to Japan to re-equip with Ki-67 'Peggy' bombers. The 62nd initially relocated to Jesselton airfield for the flight home, and on 16 December crews were ready to take off in two Ki-49s, eager to see Japan again after a long time away in Southeast Asia. The upbeat atmosphere was suddenly interrupted by air raid sirens after a solitary B-24 was spotted heading in a southerly direction at medium altitude.

After a while, when things had calmed down, the first bomber, flown by 1Lt Naga, started taxiing out to the runway, followed by the 'Helen' of WO Inoue. Moments later, the wail of the air raid sirens filled the air once again. Groundcrews had been standing on the edge of the runway waving the departing bombers goodbye when three P-38s suddenly appeared and started shooting up the two helpless bombers. Naga's Ki-49 had just taken off when it was badly hit, causing the aircraft to crash into the sea. Inoue's 'Helen' was also targeted, the bomber catching fire as it accelerated for take-off. The aircraft overshot the end of the runway and was burnt out.

In just one pass, the USAAF fighters had destroyed both Donryu, the trio of P-38s from the 18th FG based on Morotai having been lurking behind a small mountain near Jesselton awaiting the reconnaissance report from the B-24 before launching their devastating attack.

The following day (17 December), one after another, the remaining 'Helens' (carrying 50 aircrew between them) departed Borneo and flew to Saigon, in French Indochina. Here, personnel spent 48 hours recuperating – many of them enjoyed watching American films at local theatres. After making a stop at Hainan Island on 19 December, the unit landed at Kagi airfield on Formosa, where it handed the 'Helens' over to the local aviation arsenal. Aircrew finally reached Fusa, in Tokyo, on New Year's Day, where they were issued with factory-fresh Ki-67s.

74th AND 95th SENTAI

Aside from the 62nd Sentai, two other units equipped with the Ki-49 were also committed to the ill-fated defence of the Philippines. Both the 74th and 95th Sentai had been formed in Manchuria in December 1942, the former at Gongzhuling on the 20th and the latter at Zhendong some 48 hours earlier. They were issued with early-build Ki-49s, with the 74th initially having only enough personnel and aircraft to equip two chutai – the unit eventually received an additional 100 air- and groundcrew from the 7th Sentai in May 1943, allowing it to become a full three-chutai sentai. Designated a heavy bomber training unit, the 95th was equipped with both Ki-21s and Ki-49s.

Having seen no action for more than a year in Manchuria, both sentai were posted to Japan (the 74th relocated to Mito and the 95th went to Hokota, both in Ibaraki Prefecture) in February 1944 and assigned maritime patrol duties.

This 74th Sentai Model 2 Otsu Donryu was one of the very few Ki-49s to be equipped with Taki-1 air-to-surface vessel (ASV) radar. The bomber was also fitted with multiple exhausts to both dampen the flames during night sorties and provide extra boost from the engines (*Author's Collection*)

Col Kojiro Ogawa, who led the 5th Hikodan during the defence of the Philippines, was a very capable and experienced commander and one of the few IJAAF officers who specialised in heavy bomber operations (*Author's Collection*)

A month later, they were transferred to Hokkaido (Japan's second largest island), from where they patrolled the waters around the Kurile Islands and the Sea of Okhotsk. Apart from undertaking these uneventful missions, both squadrons emphasised night bombing training and practised skip bombing and broadside attacks against surface vessels. Crews gradually improved their flight performance, becoming highly proficient in the operation of the 'Helen' as a result.

In September 1944, the 5th Hikodan, to which both sentai were assigned, was ordered to task all of the aircraft under its command to transport duties. The 'Helens' had to fly the maintenance crews and equipment of the 1st, 11th and 22nd Sentai (all fighter units equipped with the brand new Nakajima Ki-84 'Frank'), as well as the headquarters personnel of the 12th Hikodan to which the fighter sentai belonged, to the Philippines. These units would subsequently participate in Operation *Sho-1*.

From 2–9 October, the 74th and the 95th Sentai, each equipped with 15 aircraft, airlifted 56 groundcrew of the 1st Sentai, as well as their equipment and provisions, from Kashiwa, in Chiba Prefecture, to Clark Field, making stops at Hamamatsu, Nyutabaru (Miyazaki Prefecture), Shanghai and Chiayi. All the aircraft successfully completed their flights bar the bomber flown by 1Lts Higashi and Azuma, which flew into a hill in Chiba. All on board were killed. Two more airlifts involving five 'Helens' were undertaken between 18–25 October.

On 1 November the 5th Hikodan was attached to the 4th Kokugun and ordered to take part in the defence of the Philippines. The 5th had been led by Col Kojiro Ogawa from 22 September, while the commanders of the 74th and 95th Sentai, Lt Cols Kaminuma and Osawa, were ex-infantry officers. Having both taken charge in April 1944, they possessed no knowledge or experience in the operation of aircraft. They duly gave free rein to the chutai commanders while trying to familiarise themselves with the Ki-49 during the units' time at Hokkaido.

Conversely, Col Ogawa was one of the most experienced aviation officers in the IJAAF and an expert in heavy bomber operations. Having graduated from the IJA Officers Academy in 1918, he was immediately involved in the development of bomber aircraft and the establishment of the units formed to fly them. Following service with the 7th Rentai, Ogawa joined the technical department of the IJAAF Headquarters before becoming an instructor with the Hamamatsu heavy bomber school in 1931. He was involved in the purchase and transportation of Fiat BR.20 bombers from Italy to Japan in 1937–38, and in March 1940 Ogawa became sentai commander of the most battle-hardened jubakutai in the IJAAF, the 60th Sentai. In light of the inexperience of the appointed sentai commanders, he was basically in charge of both the 74th and the 95th Sentai.

When the 5th Hikodan received orders to the Philippines, the headquarters had one aircraft and 60 personnel, the 74th Sentai was equipped with 28 aircraft and 460 air- and groundcrew and the 95th Sentai had 27 aircraft and 420 personnel. On 6 November a small contingent that included the two sentai commanders flew to Del Carmen airfield, on Luzon, to make all the necessary preparations for the redeployment of the units. Four days later, the 74th Sentai's 28 Ki-49s took off from Utsunomiya aviation arsenal and reached Del Carmen airfield, their base of operations, on 15 November.

Upon their arrival, unit personnel were dismayed to find the base, originally constructed by the USAAC as part of the Clark Field complex, defenceless against air attacks. All requests for anti-aircraft artillery were rejected as there were no units to spare, and emergency airfields for the bombers to be dispersed to during air raids could not be allotted at the time. The small forests around the airfield could conceal a handful of fighters, but a large number of bombers would have been next to impossible to hide. Regardless, the crews had to work around the clock trying to camouflage the Ki-49s, cutting down fresh tree branches every two days so that the older brown leaves would not stand out among the green of the forest canopy. Every single drop of fuel also had to be drained from the tanks and fuel lines to make the aircraft less likely to catch fire during strafing attacks.

In spite of such efforts, these measures were wholly inadequate to prevent the disaster that befell the 74th on 19 November – a mere four days after the unit had arrived in the Philippines. At 0700 hrs, approximately 30 carrier-based US Navy aircraft suddenly appeared in the sky over Del Carmen. Initially, pilots carried out with cautious high-altitude attacks due to their apprehension about possible anti-aircraft guns defending the airfield. When they realised there was in fact no opposition, the pilots strafed the area and released their bombs, the latter blowing away the tree cover and leaving the Ki-49s totally exposed. By the time the attack finally ended at 1300 hrs, nine 'Helens' had been destroyed and four more seriously damaged. However, the aircraft hidden in the northern part of the airfield had not been spotted and were therefore intact.

Any hope the 74th had of escaping further destruction evaporated ten minutes later when a second wave of 40 US Navy aircraft commenced a ferocious attack against the Ki-49s hidden in the forest to the north of Del Carmen. When the second raid was over, only two 'Helens' remained intact. Subsequent waves of enemy aircraft targeted the fuel depot near the sentai barracks, with drums exploding and buildings being set on fire. Eventually the enemy aircraft returned to their carriers at 1830 hrs.

Two Ki-49s that had been expected to arrive at 1730 hrs from Taiwan hurriedly escaped into the clouds upon seeing the attack from the air. They waited for the enemy aircraft to depart the area before landing. Once on the ground, they joined the 74th Sentai's aircrew in lamenting the loss of the unit's aircraft, including six bombers equipped with Taki-1 search radar. On a positive note, the 74th had suffered no casualties, and the aircrew were hopeful that they would be back in action soon once replacement aircraft had arrived.

The 95th Sentai enjoyed better luck, its aircrew having departed Tachikawa with 27 'Helens' on 17 November. They duly reached Clark

This photograph, taken in November 1944 at Chiayi airfield on Formosa, features a 95th Sentai Donryu and its crew just prior to relocating to Clark Field in the Philippines. In the back row, from left to right, are 2Lt Kuribayashi, sentai commander Lt Col Osawa and Maj Sueo Yamamoto, commander of the 1st Chutai. In front of them are, from left to right, WO Matsui, Sgt Maj Yanagidate and Sgt Matsuoka (*Author's Collection*)

Field East two days later. Groundcrew from both sentai, together with the headquarters officers of the 5th Hikodan, travelled to the Philippines by ship. When Col Ogawa was briefed of the disaster at Del Carmen, he ordered the 95th to give ten of its 'Helens' to the 74th, thus bringing some parity between the two units.

Having taken into consideration the performance of the Ki-49 during previous operations in New Guinea, Burma and the Philippines, the lack of combat experience amongst the aircrew of both sentai and the overwhelming aerial strength of the opposition, Ogawa and his staff officers concluded that attacks during daylight hours would only bring about more losses for no tangible results. Night missions flown by proficient pilots guiding less experienced crews were expected to have a better chance of success, keeping casualties to a minimum.

The first such operation was scheduled for 22 November, but unfavourable weather led to its postponement until the following night. The main targets were the invasion beachhead and the airfield at Tacloban, the provincial capital of Leyte. With the 'Helen's' cruising speed of 270 km/h, it would take about six hours to complete the round trip between Clark and Leyte. Radio direction finders were available to help crews navigate in the dark. Reconnaissance aircraft had also provided plenty of photographs to both units, which meant that they were well informed about the enemy positions and the general topography of the area.

On the night of 23 November, three 'Helens' from the 74th Sentai loaded with ten 50-kg bombs apiece managed to complete their mission, starting a number of fires in the target area before returning to base without any mishaps. 2Lt Tamotsu Oishi was serving with the unit as a pilot and commander of the 3rd Chutai at the time, and he provided the following account of the 74th's first raid;

'In the morning, the flight plan was formulated. We received an aerial photo of Tacloban Field, and upon closer inspection we could see the enemy aeroplanes lined up on the runway. This was our target! I memorised all the information from the available photos and maps, which gave me confidence that we could successfully complete this mission. I had a peaceful sleep in the afternoon and woke up at 1630 hrs. Finally, we were participating in a combat mission! First, I took a bath and changed into fresh clothes. At dinner, only the crews on a mission were served a special meal consisting of eggs and canned crab. That supper was exceptional.

'Although it was very hot on the ground, prior to boarding the bomber you had to don a jacket underneath your flying suit so as to stay warm at high altitude. And the whole attire got heavier if you had to carry a pistol and a sword.

'It was 1900 hrs when all the crews finally gathered in front of the sentai commander's office. After getting briefed about the weather, the locations of enemy aircraft en route, precautions to observe during flight and more, we travelled to the airfield by car. The bomber I was assigned had arrived 30 minutes earlier from San Marcelino airfield [where all 74th Sentai aircraft were hidden following the disastrous attack on 19 November], and I was briefed about its condition, the bomb-aiming equipment, the ordnance that had been loaded, the condition of the engines and the serviceability of the machine guns.

'Our crew gathered together, and we were greeted by our commander [3rd Chutai CO Capt Tamotsu Nakata] and treated to a cup of sake. His last words were, "Start the engines in ten minutes. Fall out".

'The departure of the first bomber was scheduled for 2100 hrs, with the following aircraft scheduled to take off one after another at intervals of ten to 15 minutes. When Capt Nakata's aeroplane commenced taxiing, all those who had gathered at the side of the runway started cheering.

'Our crew boarded the aeroplane and I gave the order to start the engines. I had a feeling that we were not going to come back. The inertia starter of the left engine began to rotate. With the command "Ignition!", the right engine came to life. After a particularly careful test run, we could hear the cheers from the runway. The chocks were removed and we started taxiing, at which point we heard the cries of "Oishi banzai [hurrah!]" rising like a storm. I was electrified and kept shouting "Let's do it! Let's go!"

'Our bomber reached the runway holding position markers, at which point the radio operator received the message that we were cleared for take-off. I waved one last time, closed the canopy, shouted "Let's go!" without thinking and pulled the control column all the way towards me. The aircraft, with a bombload of 1000-kg, was quite heavy, and we left the ground at the edge of the take-off marker. I quickly looked off to the side of the bomber and saw that there were still comrades on the runway cheering us on.

'We slowly climbed while following a course to Tacloban. The radio operator reported "Commander, it's the end of radio communications". We kept climbing to 3000, 4000, 5000 m. The bright moonlight illuminated the area. We could see the lights of Manila on our port side, and the coastline was clearly visible. I had some food to keep myself awake, but I could hardly taste it. The maps and our course took all my attention.

A formation of 95th Sentai 'Helens' flies over Luzon Strait (more commonly known to Japanese pilots as Bashi Channel) between Formosa and Luzon, this body of water connecting the Philippine Sea with the South China Sea in the western Pacific Ocean. This photograph was taken on 19 November 1944, when the unit was relocating to Clark Field. Note that the slanting and combat bands of the 1st Chutai Ki-49 Model 2 Otsu in the foreground do not wrap around the entire fuselage (*Author's Collection*)

I ordered the crew to "Turn off all the lights. Everyone, rest as much as possible".

'At 0030 hrs, Leyte Island finally came into view. By then my crew was nervous as we approached our target, and I quickly told them, "Everyone, go to your battle stations. Be on your guard!" There was already a fire burning on Tacloban, probably because of Nakata's bombs [his "Helen" was flying immediately ahead of Oishi's].

'Then we started a slow descent at a speed of 350 km/h. I held back my excitement and looked through the bombsight [by then Oishi would have moved to the bombardier's position in the nose of the aircraft, as it was his job to drop the ordnance on target]. I could clearly see the "bubble" [the internal sighting system of the Type 88 bombsight incorporated a bubble as a sighting index], but I wasn't as calm as I would have liked. I gave some adjustment commands to the pilot. "It's a little to the right. That's it, okay, stay in that direction. Yes, stay on that path. Okay, okay. I'm dropping the bombs!", followed by "All bombs have been released, bank to the right and increase speed". Everyone was focused. I had no time to feel scared. The flak looked beautiful like fireworks. One burst nearby brought me back to reality. It is only when you are free of tension that you feel a bit scared. "What the hell! Do they really think they can hit us with this flak?"

'We kept climbing, and as I looked down I saw that the first bomb had fallen near the coastline and then 20 bombs hit a supply depot and the aeroplane distribution area one after the other. They fell in a straight line, and I saw them exploding and spitting fire. They were fragmentation bombs containing both explosives and incendiary bullets, and more than a dozen small blazes erupted. The largest was probably at the fuel depot.

'Our radio operator sent a message back to Del Carmen by wireless, reporting that "the Oishi bomber has completed its attack successfully and is ready to return". With the sending of this message, we felt that our mission was half over, but the enemy nightfighter attack we were so worried about came about 20 minutes later. There was no way our heavy bomber could match the speed of a nightfighter, and the enemy aircraft was getting closer and closer. Blue lines of tracers passed over our heads – the fighter was shooting at us from behind and had us at a disadvantage. "Watch out in the back!" I shouted shortly after the tail gunner started shooting like crazy. I flew at high speed in the direction of nearby clouds and the enemy fighter lost us. My heart was still racing when we eventually came back out of the clouds.

'We all remained quiet until somebody said "I'm hungry" over the intercom and the tension in the cabin gradually eased.'

Further missions (detailed below) were flown by both sentai through to the end of the month and into early December, with bombers mainly targeting the Allied-held airfield of Tacloban and nearby artillery positions and depots.

LEYTE BOMBING MISSIONS				
Date	Unit (and number of aircraft involved)	Target	Bombload	Result and notes
23/11	74th (x3)	Tacloban airfield	30 x 50-kg Ta-Dan cluster bombs	Each aircraft bombed from a different direction at ten-minute intervals. Large fire seen
24/11	95th (x6)	Tacloban airfield	40 x 50-kg 2 x 500-kg	Damaged the runway, fire seen in many places
25/11	95th (x2)	Tacloban airfield	Ta-Dan cluster bombs	Attack from altitude of 100 m. Two aircraft lost
26/11	74th (x6)	Tacloban airfield	60 x 50-kg	Two aircraft lost, one on return to base – crash-landed in the sea and crew rescued by hospital ship. One very low-level strafing attack, front gunner killed
27/11	74th (x6)	Carigara depot and artillery base	60 x 50-kg	One lost
28/11	95th (x?)	Tacloban airfield		
29/11	74th (x3)	Carigara artillery base	30 x 50-kg	
30/11	95th (x2)	Tacloban airfield	20 x 50-kg	One lost
1/12	74th (x3)	Carigara artillery base	30 x 50-kg	
5/12	74th (x2)	Dulag airfield (x1) Burauen airfield (x1)	20 x 50-kg	Damage to searchlights at Dulag airfield

During these raids, no 'Helens' fell victim to enemy anti-aircraft fire or nightfighters. All losses were due to poor weather conditions, navigation miscalculations or communication problems with the radio detection finding stations. All in all, between 23 November and 5 December, a single 'Helen' from the 74th Sentai crash-landed and three failed to return to base, resulting in a total of 22 casualties. Two bombers from the 95th Sentai also crash-landed, one failed to return and two more were destroyed in accidents, resulting in the unit suffering 20 casualties.

OPERATION *TE*

While US forces were making slow but steady progress against the IJA on Leyte, Gen Tomoyuki Yamashita, the overall commander of Japanese forces in the Philippines, emphasised the need to prevent the development of airfields that had already fallen into enemy hands, as these could sever the lines of communication between Japan and the oil rich NEI. Nevertheless, the night attacks mounted by the IJAAF bombers on the airfields proved to be nothing more than a nuisance to the Allies,

A group of Takachiho paratroopers study a terrain board as they are briefed on details of the impending Operation *Te* raid (*Author's Collection*)

yielding only meagre results as the enemy's air superiority began to exact a heavy toll on the IJA.

Following in the footsteps of the highly successful parachute assault on the airfields of Palembang, in the NEI, in February 1942, the IJA hastily devised a series of plans to attack a number of airfields in eastern Leyte in order to hinder their use by Allied air forces. These operations called not only for the dropping of paratroopers onto the enemy airfields, but also for a number of aircraft carrying troops to land and obstruct Allied operations on the runways. Ki-49s would play a supporting role.

A first attempt was made on the night of 26–27 November, when the 4th Kokugun sent the 1st Guerrilla Company of the Kaoru Airborne Raiding Detachment against Buri (also known as Burauen North) and Bayung (Burauen South) airfields. Four Kawasaki Ki-56 'Thalia' transports (based on licence-built Lockheed 14 twin-engined aircraft) carrying 40 raiders between them attempted to approach Leyte, but all bar one was shot down over Burauen by anti-aircraft fire and none actually reached their target. Despite these losses, the 4th Kokugun HQ opted to mount a second raid, as neutralising the airfields was deemed to be of the utmost importance.

This time, the 3rd and part of the 4th Teishin Rentai (Raiding Regiment) under the overall command of Maj Tsuneharu Shirai were assigned a much more complicated and expanded mission. The targets were the same as for the previous ill-fated operation, with the addition of San Pablo airfield. Six Mitsubishi Ki-57 'Topsy' transports were assigned to the Buri attack, with 17 more allocated to Bayung and just three to San Pablo. Once these airfields were secured by the paratroopers, they were to be reinforced by the 26th Infantry Division after it had traversed the mountain range between Burauen and Ormoc.

The airborne element of the raid was codenamed Operation *Te* (after the general name for all IJA parachute units, teishin), with the transport element being nicknamed the 'Takachiho Unit' after a town in central Kyushu. The overall operation, which included the ground elements, was codenamed Operation *Wa*.

Following the initial parachute drops, more were planned with heavy equipment, supplies and the remaining paratroopers that could not be carried by the limited number of transports available. There was concern that these follow-up flights could be hampered

Takachiho raiders assigned to the attack on Tacloban airfield line up at Clark Field in front of their Donryu transport to listen to a final speech from their commanding officer. They are all wearing life jackets but no parachutes (*Author's Collection*)

by enemy aircraft based at the airfields of Tacloban and Dulag, so the plan grew to include attacks on these bases as well. Seven Ki-57s were assigned to drop paratroopers on Dulag and two on Tacloban.

Furthermore, two Ki-49s from the 74th Sentai and two from the 95th were to belly-land in the middle of the runways at both airfields to further disrupt operations. Once the aircraft had come to a halt, the paratroopers would spring into action from the 'Helen' transports to wreak mayhem and destruction for as long as they could. Although theirs was deemed to be a suicide mission, the original plan provided retreat options into the mountains northwest of Tacloban. All the 'Helen' transports could carry ten raiders and had a crew of one pilot and one engineer, and the aircraft assigned to belly-land at the two target airfields also included a radio operator.

The 35-strong Ki-57 force, commanded by Col Keigo Kawashima, came from the 1st Teishin (Raiding) Sentai, christened the 'Kirishima Unit', and one chutai from the 2nd Teishin Sentai, known as the 'Aso Unit'. Both were named after mountains in Japan, and each Ki-57 could carry 12 paratroopers.

Unlike with previous IJA airborne operations, this time, no aircraft were assigned to drop weapons and supplies for the paratroopers, so each soldier, who was already equipped with a ten-kilogramme Type 4 parachute, had to carry an additional 30-kg load that included not only his personal weapon, but ammunition and food for three days as well. The raiders in the 'Helen' transports did not carry parachutes, of course, and they were supplied with extra ammunition and explosives instead.

According to the plan, following the initial drop, the Ki-57 transports were to return to their bases and a second mission was to be flown by 'Topsys' loaded up with heavy weapons for the paratroopers that had already been dropped. Finally, a third wave of Ki-57s would then fly in an additional 80 paratroopers. If conditions did not allow the follow-on missions to be undertaken on the same day as the initial drops, they were to be rescheduled for the following days.

The commander of the raiders seen in the previous photograph was 1Lt Sato, a karate master born in Okinawa who had a distinctive moustache. Here, he presents arms in front of a transport Donryu. The belly-landing attacks on Tacloban and Dulag were suggested by Sato (*Author's Collection*)

Immediately prior to the first drop, six 'Helens' from the 74th and seven from the 95th Sentai, under the overall command of Maj Yamamoto of the latter unit, were to release smoke bombs on Buri, Bayung and San Pablo airfields to obscure the descent of the parachutists. The Ki-49s were to then return to their bases for reloading with bombs, after which they were to attack enemy positions on the airfields and support the paratroopers on the ground.

The whole air armada was to be escorted by around 30 fighters from the 13th, 20th and 31st Sentai, under the overall leadership of Maj Susumu Nishi, CO of the latter unit. The original plan also called for every serviceable fighter at Clark Field to relocate to Negros Island, from where they were to meet the transports mid-way to Leyte. Further air support was to be provided by light bomber units equipped with Ki-48s, which were to attack enemy anti-aircraft batteries and cut the road that connected Burauen with San Pablo. It is unclear if enough 'Lilys' were ever found to carry out this part of the plan.

On D-Day – 6 December – last-minute adjustments were made a few hours before take-off after the pilots of all nine Ki-57s assigned to the Dulag and Tacloban airfield attacks declared their commitment to belly-land with their aircraft. This meant that all the 'Topsys' were now reassigned to the Dulag operation, and the four 'Helen' transports would land at Tacloban.

At 1540 hrs, the 35 Ki-57s and the Ki-49s from the 95th Sentai, escorted by 30 fighters, commenced taking off from Clark Field. Overhead Manila, they formed up with six 'Helens' from the 74th Sentai based at Del Carmen airfield and, further south, they were joined by more fighters over Negros Island. It was an impressive site, and the last time the IJAAF would make such a show of force over the Philippines. The formation headed to the southern tip of Leyte Island, before making a sharp turn to the north and, shortly after, splitting up into separate groups bound for Burauen and Tacloban.

While flying near the east coast of Leyte Island, the 'Topsys' and 'Helens' tasked with crash-landing at Tacloban and Dulag passed directly over more than 100 US Navy vessels supporting the landings. The anti-aircraft fire thrown up by the warships was so fierce that all the Ki-49s and Ki-57s were shot down – a few pilots managed to crash-land just offshore.

The parachute drops were more successful, even though anti-aircraft fire was again intense. The paratroopers had started jumping from the transports at 1800 hrs, just minutes before sunset. With the airfields soon enveloped in darkness, the situation on the ground became confusing for both sides. A small group of six paratroopers led by Maj Shirai landed on the eastern side of Buri airfield and attacked parked aircraft, installations, fuel and ammunition dumps. More paratroopers gradually joined the group, swelling its number to about 60, and at midnight they dug in in the forest on the northern side of the runway.

The group that was to be dropped over Bayung airfield mistakenly jumped over San Pablo instead, and a large gathering of around 200 paratroopers assembled at either end of the runway. As with the attack on Buri airfield, they targeted aircraft, installations and provisions, spreading panic among US troops.

Meanwhile, the surviving 'Topsys' from this initial drop headed back to Lipa airfield to load up with heavy weapons. No more than 20 remained following the first operation, and all of them had been riddled with anti-aircraft fire. Four were hastily repaired, and they took off again after midnight – one immediately crashed, however. At 0200 hrs four more managed to leave Lipa, only to encounter bad weather mid-way to Leyte that forced them all to return to Angeles airfield.

The 13 'Helens' that dropped smoke bombs encountered numerous problems after successfully completing their initial mission. Three aircraft from the 74th Sentai got lost in bad weather on the way back to Clark Field and were forced to ditch in Manila Bay. Of the unit's remaining three Ki-49s that took part in the mission, only the aircraft commanded by Capt Uchida was able to refuel, reload with bombs and take off for Leyte. However, he too encountered bad weather mid-way to the target and had to abandon the mission. Uchida and his crew then got lost whilst trying to return to Clark due to miscalculations with the direction-finding system, and they were forced to crash-land on Mindoro Island. The crew was rescued five days later.

The 'Helens' from the 95th Sentai fared rather better, although they too experienced some mishaps. Having dropped their smoke bombs, the four Ki-49s under the command of Maj Yamamoto returned to Delmonte Field and were loaded with delayed-action ordnance. Having subsequently attacked Tacloban, they safely returned to base.

The three 'Helens' under the command of Capt Maruyama were scheduled to land at Clark Field, but fog over the base forced them to divert to Mabarakat. While there, they were refuelled and bombed-up, only for one of the aircraft to crash immediately after take-off. Its crew managed to escape the wreckage, although tail gunner Sgt Jingu was still in the aircraft when its bombload exploded – he had almost certainly been knocked unconscious when the Ki-49 crashed. Capt Maruyama and the remaining aircraft pressed on to the target, only to encounter bad weather en route. They duly returned to Clark.

The fact that the same 13 'Helens' had been tasked with flying ground support night bombing sorties following their smoke bombing missions to Buri, Bayung and San Pablo indicates that only a very small number of Ki-48s, if any, took part in Operation *Te*.

At 0830 hrs the following morning, a force of about 350 US troops engaged the Shirai group at Buri, leaving the Japanese paratroopers with only half their original strength. With no reinforcements arriving and no means to communicate with other units, they chose to retreat in a southerly direction in an effort to join either the 16th or 26th Divisions.

In this still taken from a cine film shot on 6 December 1944, a 2nd Chutai Ki-49 of the 95th Sentai takes off from Clark Field at the start of Operation *Te*. On board were 1Lt Sato and nine raiders bound for Tacloban airfield. All the Donryu tasked with belly-landing there were from the 2nd Chutai, whose aircraft had a red diagonal band on the rear fuselage and red propeller spinners. The white and red bands on the rudder trim tab probably indicated that this particular machine was the leader's aircraft. Note that it is a Model 2 with multiple exhausts (*Author's Collection*)

At San Pablo, the larger group that had gathered at the northern end of the airfield relocated to Buri, while the paratroopers at the southern end managed to fend off an assault by US forces. Repeated attacks by the latter finally succeeded in crushing all Japanese resistance at the southern end, while the northern group eventually established contact with elements of the 16th Division, whereupon they were told disheartening news. US forces had landed in nearby Ormoc Bay and, as a result, Operation *Wa* had been called off. Now, they would have to cross the mountains and join the battle near the landing site. For the next five days the paratroopers fought overwhelming US forces, and only a handful of survivors managed to reach Ormoc Bay.

Meanwhile, the Shirai group had continued to search the jungle for other paratroopers or infantry divisions of the IJA. Finally, on 18 December, some 12 days after the initial landing at Buri, contact was made with an element of the 26th Division and the paratroopers were told that *Wa* had been abandoned. Only 12 had survived the ordeal to that point, and their troubles were far from over. It would take them another week to reach Ormoc Bay and the headquarters of the 35th Army, which was defending the area.

During Operation *Wa*, paratroopers had attacked multiple targets on the airfields, setting fire to installations, fuel dumps, liaison aircraft and vehicles. The US Army units that engaged them were elements of the 11th Airborne Division, supported by the 38th, 96th, 149th and 382nd Infantry Divisions, which had hastily mustered groups of support and service troops. According to official US Army historical records, the paratroopers 'destroyed minor fuel and supply dumps, and a few American aircraft'. However, Japanese sources optimistically stated that 41 P-38s and 24 other fighters, six C-47 Skytrain transports, 27 L-5 Sentinel liaison aircraft and other types had been destroyed. Furthermore, 12 tanks, 42 trucks, five cars, three anti-aircraft artillery pieces and 55 installations, fuel and ammunition dumps had also been destroyed.

In retrospect, the whole operation was hampered from the very beginning by the air superiority that the Allies enjoyed over Leyte. This in turn prevented the IJAAF from undertaking any parachute drops during daylight hours, as enemy fighters were constantly patrolling the skies over the island. When the paratroopers landed in the dark, it was inevitable that they would have difficulty in assembling in order to coordinate their attacks. A complete lack of portable radios further hindered operations once on the ground. Splitting the force up in order to simultaneously drop paratroopers on three targets, instead of focusing on one airfield, was also a grave tactical error.

The audacious plan to crash-land aircraft on Tacloban was scuppered by a lack of sufficient up-to-date intelligence relating to the location of enemy vessels. Prior to Operation *Te*, both the IJAAF and the IJNAF had lost hundreds of fighters and bombers to unforgiving anti-aircraft fire in failed aerial attacks on Allied warships supporting the liberation of Leyte. It was common knowledge that flying directly over the enemy fleet meant certain death. Had the Ki-49 and Ki-57 units involved in the Tacloban raid known where the fleet was prior to take-off, they would not have chosen a flightpath that brought them directly into the sights of the enemy guns.

Finally, the extremely limited ground attack missions flown by the IJAAF in an effort to neutralise enemy anti-aircraft artillery immediately prior to the paratroopers dropping on the airfield were a total failure. Indeed, using Ki-49 heavy bombers to lay a smoke screen was little more than an act of desperation. The defenceless transports and their human cargo suffered heavy losses as a direct result. While the paratroopers were able to inflict substantial damage at two airfields, in the end, their daring, desperate exploits did little to hinder US forces as they advanced across Leyte.

ORMOC

To reinforce the small number of IJA units fighting in the Ormoc Bay area, 500 paratroopers of the 4th Raiding Regiment still in Angeles were dropped onto Valencia airfield (which remained in Japanese hands), north of Ormoc Bay.

The 'Helens' of the 74th and 95th Sentai also mounted attacks on US Navy warships in Ormoc Bay on 8 December when three Ki-49s from the 74th and four from the 95th sortied on a skip bombing mission. From the 74th, the bomber of 1Lt Miyazaki failed to locate the enemy fleet due to poor weather and returned to base. The Ki-49s of 1Lts Arifuku and Kuwahara spent more than an hour looking for their target before sending back messages that they were about to attack. Neither aircraft was ever heard from again. Maj Yamamoto from the 95th was able to spot a US Navy landing craft unloading near the shore. During the Ki-49's first pass its ordnance could not be released from the bomb-bay. The 'Helen' gained altitude, banked around and made a second pass. This time, two 250-kg bombs were released in quick succession, and the first one exploded off to the side of the vessel and the second hit the deck and bounced into the sea.

Capt Noguchi's bomber was flying with Yamamoto's aircraft. While attacking from an altitude of less than 300 m, the Ki-49 was hit by multiple rounds from a Bofors 40 mm anti-aircraft battery and crashed. A third 'Helen' in the formation, flown by WO Okawara, suffered a similar fate. The last bomber from the 95th Sentai, flown by Sgt Maj Sakai, became lost en route to the target area and ran into a solitary B-24. During a lengthy exchange between the two bombers, gunners on board the 'Helen' expended all their ammunition but failed to shoot the Liberator down.

Although the Ki-49 in turn received 48 hits from the USAAF bomber's multiple 0.50-cal machine guns, the crew managed to nurse the 'Helen' back to base.

'KIKUSUI TOKUBETSU KOGEKI-TAI'

Having effectively gained control of Leyte, the Allies turned their attention to Mindoro Island, in the central Philippines, from 12 December. Airfields subsequently built here would provide bases for USAAF fighter squadrons that would come to dominate the skies over Luzon Island, with its capital of Manila, to the north. Aircraft flying from Mindoro would also be able to stop all efforts to reinforce the Japanese garrison on Luzon from Formosa, thus isolating the forces remaining in the Philippines.

The US Sixth Army, which was tasked with undertaking the amphibious assault on Mindoro, was to be transported to the island by the Western Visayan Task Force, escorted by warships of the Seventh Fleet. The latter (specifically Task Unit 77.12.7, commanded by Rear Admiral Felix B Stump) provided cover for the vulnerable troop transports, with fighter aircraft being embarked in six escort carriers that were in turn protected by three battleships, six cruisers and many other destroyers and destroyer escorts – all of which bristled with anti-aircraft batteries.

On 12 December, the US ships set sail from Dulag, on the east coast of Leyte, bound for Mindoro via Surigao Strait. The IJA and IJN headquarters in Manila were soon made aware of the imminent threat, although they were uncertain as to the true intentions of the large US force. In spite of that, the 4th Kokugun under the command of Lt Gen Kyoji Tominaga, also based in Manila, decided to attack the US fleet with any means possible.

On 13 December, the 5th Hikodan, controlling the 74th and 95th Sentai, received orders from the 4th Kokugun instructing it to organise a 'tokubetsu kogeki-tai' (special attack, i.e. suicide, unit) to participate

Aircrew of the 'Kikusui Tokubetsu Kogeki-tai' have their last meal prior to taking off from Clark Field on the fateful mission of 14 December 1944 (*Author's Collection*)

in the overall effort to target the advancing US fleet the following day. Such attacks had been taking place on a formal and organised basis since 25 October. Seven 'Helens' from the 95th and two from the 74th were chosen for the mission, which was to be led by Capt Yoshimasa Maruyama, commander of the 2nd Chutai of the 95th Sentai. The 'special attack' unit was named 'Kikusui', based on the war banner featuring a chrysanthemum flower (kiku) floating on running water (sui) of the 14th century samurai Masashige Kusunoki, who famously had said 'I wish I had seven lives to give for my country'.

Col Ogawa, commanding the 5th Hikodan, tried to delay the operation, knowing full well that a daylight attack against six heavily defended escort carriers had absolutely no chance of success. Nevertheless, the headquarters of the 4th Hikoshiden, which had organised the whole mission, insisted that the attack take place on the 14th due to the operational availability of aircraft from other units, such as those providing escort fighters.

Sgt Nakamura was a member of the 95th Sentai at the time, and he vividly recalled the events of that fateful day;

'I will never forget the night of 13 December 1944.

I was resting in the Clark Field barracks when I heard duty officer Capt Yamauchi announce in a loud voice, "Here's the crew list for tomorrow's mission. Lead bomber: Capt Maruyama, Sgt Tachibana. No 2 bomber, Commander: 2Lt Aihara, Sgt Nakamura. No 3 . . ."

'There were no surprises in this announcement, and [although it was not confirmed as such] we all believed that this was going to be a "special attack" mission. I thought my turn had come. I sorted out my personal belongings, even though it was doubtful that they would ever reach my family. All the cigarettes I had bought in Taiwan were given out to the comrades who had taken care of me when I was suffering from dengue fever. I also wrote something like a death poem. I prayed for the health of my parents, and for my sister to become a good Japanese wife – things like that.

'After that, I donned my flightsuit and went to the sentai headquarters, where our commander read us the orders from the 5th Hikodan. "The Special Attack Unit has been named Kikusui Corps". We all shouted "Kanpai" and then drank the sake we had been presented with by Prince [Nobuhito] Takamatsu while in Obihiro. Afterwards, Capt Maruyama, the "Kikusui" commander, told us to "Sink the enemy ships without fail!", and we were all roused and inspired by his words. I had never thought that ramming and sinking an enemy ship would be a top priority when undertaking missions in the past. I considered it an act of desperation when nothing else could be done to stop the enemy.

'In our bomber, the dorsal gunner, 2Lt Aihara, was the commander, Sgt Maj Kobayashi manned the 13 mm cannon in the tail, I was the pilot, the in-flight engineer was Sgt Kawai and the radio operator was Cpl Adachi. Heavy bombers usually had two pilots, but since we were undertaking a "special attack" mission, this was considered a squandering of human resources. So, all bombers assigned such flights had only one pilot, except for the lead bomber in the formation.

'Getting the bombers ready for the mission took at least two hours. We were to be loaded with a 500-kg bomb, and with the help of groundcrewman

Sgt Maj Moriya, we managed to hang a torpedo suspension rack in the bomb-bay of the aeroplane. While I was readying the bomber for the flight, Sgt Yoshimizu came over and said, "Hey Nakamura, they all say nobody's going to return from this mission", and I replied, "Isn't that usually the fate that awaits all 'special attack unit' personnel?". He said "Really?" and walked off. Up to that point, I don't think he had actually been aware of the fate that awaited all of us.

'Once our aeroplane was finally prepared, the crew got together to discuss our course of action. I said, "Let's aim for the biggest ship we can find. We are to die anyway, so let's take with us as many enemies as we can. In the beginning, I will try to make a skip bombing attack, so, Cpl Adachi in the nose gun, hit everything you see with the 13 mm. Then I will fly over the enemy ship and, after that, I will get close to the surface of the sea. So, rear gunners, give it all you have got. If the enemy ship doesn't sink, I will turn around and crash into it. Don't forget this plan!"

'2Lt Aihara commented, "Nakamura, if possible, let's attack a small ship" [suggesting that he thought the crew would have a better chance of sinking such a vessel by conventional means, thus avoiding the need for a follow-up suicide crash]. But in their hearts, everybody thought that they were not coming back.

'Eventually, everything was ready, the test run of the engines was over and it was time to depart. At 0600 hrs on 14 December 1944, 49 of us boarded nine Donryu bombers and started to leave Clark Field. I was nervous because I was flying with a 500-kg bomb. I began taxiing to reach the starting point, opening the flaps to 15 degrees, setting the propeller pitch at its finest and fixing my gaze on Mount Arayat – our take-off mark. Next to the runway, our comrades were seeing us off, waving in the distance. I grabbed the control column, raised my right hand and yelled "Departure!" I gradually pushed the engine throttles forward, the body of my beloved aircraft shook, rushed as if it couldn't wait and kicked the ground with a final roaring sound as it took off.

'All the bombers then gathered over the airfield and headed towards Manila. There, we were supposed to join 60 escort fighters and the remnants of the "Banda-tai" [one of the first IJAAF "special attack" units to be formed, equipped with modified Ki-48-II "Lilys"].

'It was a clear day over the city. Our bomber formation slowly circled and waited a while, but there were no fighters to be seen on the horizon. In the end, our commander [Capt Maruyama] decided to set a course for our final destination – the Panay Gulf. At 3000 m, there were some cumulus clouds peculiar to the south, but the weather was fine. Bathed in the morning sunlight, the nine Donryu bombers flew on, their wings lined up tip-to-tip. After a while, the commander's aeroplane gradually lost altitude. Suddenly, when I thought that we were near our target, single red and white signal flags flew from the rear of the commander's aeroplane. It was a battle formation signal – we were finally there! I flipped up the peak of my flying cap and took my place in the battle formation.

'Our radio operator, Cpl Adachi, had by then moved to the nose gun, so communication with the other bombers was no longer possible. The formation was losing altitude and gaining speed when the dorsal and tail gunners started firing all at once. The control column got heavy, and when

I took a look, the speedometer showed 350 km/h. If I continued like this the wingtip would start to flutter, but I thought "what the hell!" and followed Capt Maruyama's bomber. When the altimeter showed 100 m, the captain's aeroplane suddenly started diving, banking sharply to the right. The speed remained at 350 km/h, and I also banked very sharply so as to keep up.

'I then spotted the sea and the shadow of an island. "Where is the enemy ship we're going to attack?" I thought for a moment, but now that the aeroplane was on the verge of stalling [after banking sharply], there really was no time to think about enemy ships. In retrospect, maybe the commander was trying to dodge attacking enemy fighters, but I wondered why all nine bombers flying in tight combat formation had to follow too. In any case, I couldn't follow Capt Maruyama's aeroplane any longer and dived under it.

'The enemy fighters attacked us moments later. My port engine was hit and started trailing black smoke. Fortunately, I was banking to the right, so I immediately increased the rotation of the right engine, reduced the propeller pitch and looked up and to my right while concentrating on flying on one engine. That's when I saw the third aeroplane in our formation, flown by Sgt Kumita, fall away trailing bright red flames and black smoke. Behind the pilot's seat, Sgt Tomita, the flight engineer, who was wearing a hinomaru headband, seemed to wave us farewell. The bomber crashed into the sea and exploded. More explosions were heard shortly thereafter, and I saw black smoke and red flames from burning fuel on the surface of the sea. Maybe these marked where the rest of our bombers had fallen after being shot down by enemy fighters?

'My aeroplane was now the only one left, and we flew near the water on one engine at a speed of 220 km/h. I couldn't turn to port because the left engine had stopped. I concentrated on flying to the right in an attempt to crash-land near an island. Engineer Sgt Kawai was desperately pushing the throttle lever of the right engine from the co-pilot's seat. Meanwhile, enemy fighters were relentlessly attacking us from above. Fireballs of yellow and red tracers were piercing my aeroplane. The noise of the enemy bullets hitting us prevented me from hearing the sound of 2Lt Aihara's 20 mm cannon firing back from the dorsal turret. I pulled the bomber up a bit to give Cpl Adachi in the nose a fighting chance with his 13 mm machine gun, but to no effect.

'Damn! I wish I was flying a fighter. I could barely keep the bomber from crashing into the sea, and while I was watching the surface of the water just below my feet, I wondered for a moment if I would die there and then. I had heard that when you're about to die the faces of your family come to mind in a flashback, but I couldn't think of anything. That's when the enemy bullets hit the cockpit. They buzzed in my ear, the compass in front of me disappeared and a few seconds later the instrument panel with all of its instruments shattered. The right wingtip then plunged into the sea and the bomber came to a violent halt.

'With seawater pouring into the cockpit with tremendous force, I took a deep breath, closed my eyes, clung to the control column, stepped on my rudder pedals and pulled as hard as I could. I thought that if I pulled on the controls, the aeroplane wouldn't sink nose first. A few seconds later, the

Donryu of the 'Kikusui Tokubetsu Kogi-tai' are waved goodbye by sentai flight- and groundcrew at Clark Field shortly after 0600 hrs on 14 December (*Author's Collection*)

bomber was floating on the surface of the water, and I spotted Sgt Kawai as he was about to jump into the sea from the left wingtip. I shouted, "Hey, Kawai! What are you doing?" He replied, "I'm going to swim to that island over there" – he took off his flying boots and jumped in the water. There was indeed something that looked like an island beyond the horizon.

'I was sitting in the cockpit and the seawater was up to my waist, so I tore up the map I had and slowly stepped out onto the left wing. All the windows in the cockpit, including the bulletproof glass which was five centimetres thick, had been blown out. The fuselage had broken in half from behind the dorsal gun, and the forward section only remained afloat because of the wings.

'At first I wondered if we had landed in the shallows, but there couldn't be any shallows in the middle of an open sea. I was not a confident swimmer, and when I was wondering what was going on around me, I heard a voice calling "Nakamura! Nakamura!" Looking around, I spotted 2Lt Aihara waving and calling me as he swam behind the wing I was standing on. The sea all around him had been dyed bright red by his blood. As soon as I reached out to pull him up, the aeroplane sank as if it was being sucked down. I went down with it, and when I resurfaced he wasn't there.

'After swimming for a while, parachutes from the sunken aeroplane came to the surface. With heaven's help, I grabbed one of them and kept floating in the water. The sky was clear and windless, and it was quiet, and it seemed like an illusion that there had been a fierce aerial battle fought overhead that morning. I heard that the enemy would shoot at survivors in the sea, but there were no signs of American aircraft in the cloudless blue sky above me.'

Nakamura was eventually rescued by Filipino guerrillas and handed over to a US Army unit. He was incarcerated in Australia as a PoW and returned to Japan post-war. Another survivor was Sgt Suito, who had been the radio operator aboard Capt Maruyama's Ki-49. No one else from the

'Kikusui' survived the ill-fated mission. The 'Helens' had been attacked by 11 P-47 Thunderbolts from the 40th FS/35th FG, the squadron's after action report mentioning;

'All the bombers were flying about 50 to 100 ft above the water. They broke up into singles and went full speed to the north. They took no evasive action and seemed to be hurrying back to the Bacolod area. The bombers were painted a greyish black and a couple were all black. They had mottled green undersurfaces. Two planes returned fire from the tail but it seemed like a fixed gun. Return fire from the turrets was very inaccurate. The guns of the Helens didn't seem to be able to fire on a high-quarter attack from the front. The Jap [sic] pilots seemed confused and gave each other no mutual fire support. Our flights broke off into individual passes and we were able to get at more of the bombers in this manner.'

In the aftermath of this mission, both the 74th and 95th Sentai were left with no bombers in serviceable condition. The following day (15 December), US forces landed unopposed on Mindoro Island. Nearby San Jose Field was immediately occupied by a US Naval Construction Battalion (Navy SeaBees), which started work on the rapid expansion of the runway and associated hardstandings.

The 15th also saw the 5th Hikodan receive orders to launch night raids against San Jose. Although the loss of 47 airmen on 14 December caused concern amongst unit commanders in-theatre, surviving aircrew showed great enthusiasm and determination when they were told of the mission. They had gained substantial combat experience and confidence during the recent fighting, and finding targets to attack on nearby Mindoro whilst flying from Clark Field would be far easier than it had been to hit airfields on faraway Leyte. Regardless, both sentai had no airworthy bombers, forcing groundcrews to work around the clock to repair Ki-49s that had sustained less serious damage.

Commencing on the night of 20 December and continuing through to the end of the month, both sentai flew nocturnal harassment missions with no more than two 'Helens' almost every night, losing just a single bomber to anti-aircraft fire during that period.

SAN JOSE FIELD NIGHT ATTACKS		
Date	Unit (and number of aircraft involved)	Result
20/12	95th (x2)	A number of fires
21/12	74th (x1)	A number of fires
22/12	95th (x2)	Large fires at different locations, hit by anti-aircraft fire at 3800m
	74th (x1)	Engine trouble, abandoned mission
23/12		Abandoned mission due to bad weather
24/12	74th (x1) 95th (x?)	Caused a large fire
25/12	74th (x1) 95th (x?)	A number of fires, destroyed airfield searchlights
26/12	74th (x1) 95th (x?)	Capt Shono's aircraft was hit by anti-aircraft fire and crash-landed back at base
27–29/12	?	
30–31/12		Abandoned missions due to bad weather

By 27 December the 74th Sentai had no operational bombers left, although it received a single example the following day. A handful of aircrew were also flown back to Japan to collect new Ki-49s for the unit. Four days later, a surprising order was received from the 3rd Kokugun directing the 5th Hikodan to relocate to Malaya to recuperate and receive reinforcements. The 3rd's area of operations was southern Burma and French Indochina, and all efforts to communicate with the 4th Kokugun met with failure. Further enquiries into what had happened to the 4th revealed that following the Allied landings on Luzon on 9 January 1945, the commander of the Kokugun, Lt Gen Tominaga, and all of his headquarters staff had taken flight to Taiwan, leaving his subordinates leaderless in the Philippines. It is little wonder that personnel controlled by the 5th Hikodan felt highly indignant about being abandoned.

The orders issued by the 3rd Kokugun stipulated that the 5th Hikodan was to prepare as many aircraft as possible to relocate from the Philippines to Pingtung, on Formosa, before being sent on to the Malayan airfield at Sungei Patani. Before leaving Clark Field for good, both Ki-49 sentai, who could only muster a handful of airworthy aircraft between them, were also tasked with the transportation of groundcrew from the fighter-equipped 13th (65 personnel) and 33rd (35 personnel) Sentai from the Philippines to Formosa. At that time, the 74th and 95th had four or five bombers each in serviceable condition. Regardless, each Ki-49 made at least six round trips through to 8 January, completing this mission without incurring any losses.

Both units were then tasked with evacuating the HQ staff officers and groundcrew of the 5th Hikodan that were still at Clark Field and also had to be evacuated to Formosa. A first effort was undertaken during the evening of 13 January, when three 'Helens' from the 74th Sentai and four from the 95th took off from Chiayi airfield on Formosa. Unfortunately, the bombers from the 95th encountered unfavourable weather en route and were forced to return to base.

The 'Helens' from the 74th reached Clark, took on board as many groundcrew as possible and were ready to return to Formosa the following day. However, on the morning of the 14th, 54 B-29 Superfortress heavy bombers from the 58th Bombardment Wing were despatched from Chengdu in Sichuan Province, China, in a devastating raid against Chiayi that destroyed the runways and airfield facilities. Fortunately for the jubakutai, only a few of its bombers were slightly damaged, although 25 personnel from the Ki-49 units were killed.

The 74th Sentai 'Helens' stranded at Clark Field had to return at a later date, and further evacuation efforts were placed on hold until Chiayi could be made operational once again. Finally, on 20 January, another transport mission was mounted with three 'Helens' from the 74th Sentai (flown by 2Lts Marukawa and Shimizu, who also led the operation, and Sgt Yokohata) and four from the 95th (flown by 1Lt Abe, who commanded the group, Sgt Majs Taniguchi and Sakai and Sgt Moriyama).

The Ki-49s started taking off from 1640 hrs, but on their way to the Philippines they were attacked by nine fighters. Shimizu sent a radio message back to Chiayi at 1752 hrs stating that the formation was going to return to base. Only two aircraft managed to make it back – Shimizu's bomber and the Ki-49 flown by Taniguchi, which limped home on the power of just its port engine. The surviving crews reported that the formation had found itself directly over an enemy fleet, and had quickly been spotted by carrier-based fighters. Shimizu and Taniguchi had sought the protection of nearby clouds, at which point they lost contact with the remaining five bombers.

The 'Helens' had been attacked by seven F4U-1D/FG-1D Corsairs from VMF-213 and five from VMF-124, both units being embarked in the aircraft carrier USS *Essex* (CV-9). The after-action report compiled by Carrier Air Group 4 described the encounter in detail;

'This 12-plane Combat Air Patrol took off at 1610 [hrs] on 20 January 1945 as TF [Task Force] 36 was entering the Ballintang Channel [also known as the Bashi Channel or Luzon Strait] between Luzon, PI, and Formosa Island and returned to base at 1820 [hrs].

'At about 1700 [hrs], the [VMF-213] flight led by [Capt R W] Kersey found four twin-engined bombers [probably the 74th Sentai group], at first thought to be Helens or Bettys, but finally decided on as Helens, at 12,000 ft. The flight had been vectored onto these bogies by base, so they attacked the enemy aircraft from a good position above and out of the sun. The first run was a complete surprise, and as the division closed from above and behind, firing, one Helen turned to port into the clouds. Kersey and [2Lt J D] Batson [of VMF-213] made three overhead runs on one Helen just northeast of DD [destroyer] picket, which reported it splashed. Going down below the clouds, Kersey, whose fire concentrated on the starboard engine, is credited with one plane destroyed.

'Kersey and Batson then picked up another Helen to starboard on a course of 270 degrees below the cloud base. Chasing him five miles to the port of DD picket, the section had to pull up into the clouds to escape AA [anti-aircraft fire] thrown up by DD picket.

'Kersey and Batson then made several beam passes, working the bomber over for several minutes. [1Lt G W] Stallings [of VMF-213] also fired into the Helen. It seems to have taken no evasive action nor tried to climb for clouds. Its speed was 160 to 170 kts [about 300km/h], and its colour was olive or greenish brown. Red meatballs were plainly seen on wings and fuselage, and the Helen was firing from the after greenhouse. Batson observed his bullets exploding into the port engine, and smoke pouring from it. He emptied all his remaining ammunition into this specific area, and Kersey, too, riddled the fuselage and port wing, yet the Helen was not observed to fall, and shortly after, beginning to smoke, disappeared into a cloud layer. Both pilots feel quite sure the Helen could not have returned to base. However, it is listed with us as a probable, credit to Batson.

'Meantime, [1Lt J D] Boutte [of VMF-213] and Stallings, picking out one of the four Helens in the original formation, gave chase. Stallings, swishing 15 degrees to either side of the Helen's tail, riddled the fuselage from tail to cockpit, and both wings, with several long bursts. Following one of these bursts, the bomber, which had been making steadily for cloud cover, fell off in a straight-down dive, apparently out of control, and it appears at that moment the pilot had been killed. Boutte followed it into the overcast and fired a burst into the plane, which was observed to crash into the sea – credit to Stallings.

'About this same time, [1Lt W] McGill [VMF-124], [2Lt P M] Kehoe [VMF-213], [1Lt R F] Strom [VMF-213] and [1Lt D A] Barberi [VMF-213] were vectored toward more bogies some 60 miles north of base. Cloud base here was about 3500 ft, with 9/10ths cover.

At 1700 [hrs], the flight from 18,000 ft tallyhoed four twin-engined bombers thought to be Sallys or Helens, and now determined to be Helens [possibly the 95th Sentai group]. The bombers, flying at 12,000 ft, scattered on sighting the interceptors, and Strom got a few bursts into one before it disappeared into the clouds. He observed no damage, and this plane was not again sighted.

'McGill, in a high-side attack on one Helen, sucked flat and fired until forced to push over or collide. The Helen was firing "20mm" from the tail turret, and as McGill closed, began throwing what appeared to be tin cans about one foot square from the tail, port side [most probably the empty magazines]. The Helen started smoking from its starboard engine and went into a portside spiral from which it never recovered [possibly Taniguchi's aircraft].

'Another Helen, following the smoking plane to port, attracted McGill's attention, and he made three high-side runs, sucking flat after each one, and firing until nearly running into the bomber. This Helen was also firing "20mm" from the tail and dropping the can-like objects – no explosion was noticed, but McGill was flying very close behind the planes. Going into the clouds with this Helen, McGill broke out at 1500 ft and saw it and the first Helen splash about half-a-mile apart, number two about 15 seconds after number one. Strom, breaking through the clouds, also verified these splashes.

'Meantime, Kehoe made a run on a Helen, breaking off as McGill took over, who splashed it. He made a run on another Helen, securing hits in the port wing from a 15-degree position above and astern. His third run commenced from a thousand feet altitude advantage, and was a tail attack on a lone Helen which was at 3000 or 4000 ft. From a position 15 degrees above and slightly to port, Kehoe concentrated on the port wing and engine, setting the area afire. The Helen was firing tracers from the after greenhouse gun but secured no hits. Falling, aflame, the bomber exploded at about 500 feet, and went into the sea. This kill was also observed by Capt Kersey.

'About 1740 [hrs], another vector was given to this flight, and one Helen was tallyhoed about 30 miles northwest of base. Strom and Barberi made overhead runs on this bandit, and believe they secured hits. Then McGill and Kehoe latched onto it, and McGill in a high-side attack sucked flat and fired until forced to pull up to avoid collision. He burned the Helen at the right wing root, and saw (as did others in the division) the Helen fall into the sea.

'These Helens were greenish brown, and large red circles were observed on the fuselage and both wingtips. No other markings were apparent.'

The report also mentions that the 'Enemy planes attempted no manoeuvre other than belated dives into the overcast. They were all slow and cumbersome by comparison. Speed about 160 kts. Diving speed, very slow and gradual. Only armament noted was tail gunner and after greenhouse gun (maybe two on Helens).'

Since the Donryu assigned to the transport mission were configured to carry as many passengers as possible back to Formosa, the 74th Sentai aircraft had only a crew of three (pilot, co-pilot and in-flight engineer, who probably also operated the dorsal 20 mm cannon), without any other gunners aboard. The 95th Sentai aircraft had four crew, possibly including tail gunners, but no waist or nose gunners. The fact that a 20 mm tail gun is mentioned in the report is somewhat puzzling. Either these were Ki-49-IIIs, of which only six prototype examples were ever built, or perhaps aircraft that had been field-modified with a single Ho-1 cannon in the tail.

As a consequence of this doomed attempt, the 5th Hikodan declared all transport missions as concluded. Nevertheless, Maj Yamamoto, who was the 1st Chutai commander of the 95th Sentai, stated that he was willing to fly again to save the groundcrew left behind. And so one final effort was made on the night of 22 January with three bombers. On the flight back to Formosa the following day, a Donryu was shot down over Tainan with the loss of nine crew and passengers.

Back on Luzon, 202 groundcrew from the 74th Sentai, 156 from the 95th Sentai and 20 staff officers from the headquarters of the 5th Hikodan were left behind. They had to take refuge from the advancing US forces by fleeing into nearby mountains, where they were ravaged by hunger and disease. Only 33 were repatriated to Japan at war's end.

Meanwhile, the losses suffered during the evacuation missions left the 5th Hikodan with next to no aircraft to execute the relocation to Malaya. At this point, Lt Col Ogawa decided to try and reorganise the two sentai, and he looked to Japan for replacement crews and bombers. Only limited numbers of both were available, and by early March the units had enough aircraft and groundcrew to finally relocate to Malaya.

On 9 March, two aircraft from the 74th and one from the 95th Sentai took off from Chiayi with the forward echelon of the hikodan on board, the latter being tasked with making the necessary arrangements for the unit transfer. They reached Sungei Patani on 11 March after making stops at Sanya airfield on Hainan Island and Phnom Penh, in present-day Cambodia. Only Ogawa had previously flown this west route, and he personally led the formation.

Just as preparations for the move had been finalised, completely out of the blue, a new message was received on 20 March ordering the 5th Hikodan to relocate to Obihiro, in Hokkaido. Five days later both sentai commenced the move to Kyushu, with three aircraft departing from Sungei Patani. By 3 April, most of the personnel had gathered at Kumamoto, in Kyushu, before finally reaching Obihiro two days later. By then, the majority of the Donryu in the units' inventory were too old and barely operational. Slowly, replacement Ki-67s arrived, together with fresh aircrew.

On 6 April Ogawa came to the decision to merge the two units into one to form a new 74th Sentai, which came under the control of the 1st Kokugun, charged with defending Japan. Two weeks later, Ogawa was reassigned as commander of the Utsunomiya aviation arsenal and Lt Col Shigeo Nomoto, formerly CO of the 12th Sentai, took charge of the 'Peggy'-equipped unit.

CHAPTER SIX

TRANSPORT DONRYU

These three 'Helens' were found at Kalidjati airfield (present-day Suryadarma AFB) in West Java following the Japanese surrender. The Donryu in the foreground are both Model 2 Otsu, as indicated by the oil cooler beneath the engine cowling and the multiple exhausts. The bomber in the background is an old Model 1, and apart from the number '78' at the base of its rudder, the aircraft seems to have an earlier unit tail marking that has been overpainted. From the shape of the latter, the aircraft belonged to the Hamamatsu school or, more likely, the Rikugun Koku Tsushin Gakko. Since no jubakutai equipped with 'Helen' bombers remained in Java during the final months of the war, these aircraft had most probably belonged to a transport unit (*Author's Collection*)

Nakajima ceased production of Donryu in December 1944. Despite high attrition, a very small number of Ki-49s remained scattered in the territories still occupied by Japanese forces, and whenever they could be returned to flyable condition, the aircraft were used as transports.

As detailed in the previous chapters of this book, some jubakutai, like the 61st and 62nd Sentai, handed over their combat-weary aircraft to local aviation arsenals, after which they were reassigned to transport units. Amongst the latter was the 7th Yuso Hikotai (Transport Unit) organised on 30 June 1941 in Yokaichi, Shiga Prefecture. It was manned by members of Manshu Koku (Manchukuo Aviation), the national airline of the vassal state of Manchukuo, and, later, by personnel from Dai Nippon Koku (Great Japan Airways), the national airline of Japan.

Initially, the unit was equipped with six Nakajima Ki-34 light transports organised into two chutai and based in Bangkok, from where they flew missions in Southeast Asia, before moving to Rangoon and flying in Burma. From 1943, the 7th Yuso Hikotai was located in Davao, on Mindanao Island, prior to transferring to Manila in September 1944. On the 21st of that month the unit lost all of its transport aircraft during a US bombing raid. It received Donryu as replacements, at which point the 7th Yuso Hikotai formed two chutai – the 11th Yuso Hiko Chutai with four 'Helens' (serial numbers 3517, 3567, 3585 and 3594), all of which were Model 2 Otsu, and the 12th Yuso Hikotai Chutai, also with four

'Helens' (Model 2 Ko 3252 and Model 2 Otsu 3446, 3471 and 3555). Finally, the unit headquarters was assigned Ki-49 3082, which was a very early production Model 2 Ko, as well as a small number of Ki-48 'Lilys' for transport and reconnaissance duties.

The 'Helens' transported provisions and personnel throughout the Philippines and on the Shanghai–Formosa–Philippines–Borneo–Singapore route. By the end of 1944, with most of the sea routes cut off by Allied submarines and the many airfields established in the Philippines having fallen to US forces, the only means of communication between mainland Japan and Southeast Asia was via the air route from Kyushu to Okinawa, then on to Formosa or Shanghai following the Chinese coastline.

'Helens' assigned to transport units helped to evacuate pilots and transfer desperately needed supplies and equipment. Naturally, these aircraft were old, sometimes far beyond their operational expiration dates, and the lack of spare parts meant that they could only fly a handful of missions.

By war's end, most of the jubakutai still operated 'Sallys', especially Model 2s, which were gradually being replaced with 'Peggys' as the IJAAF readied itself for the final showdown – the attack against the main islands of Japan. There were very few airworthy 'Helens'.

This wrecked 'Helen' was found by the US Marine Corps at Naha airfield on Okinawa following its capture in April 1945. The airfields on the island were employed as refuelling stopovers for Japanese aircraft that lacked the range to fly non-stop from Kyushu to Formosa. In early 1945, the 74th and 95th Sentai used this route when they relocated from Formosa to mainland Japan. Transport 'Helens' of the 7th Yuso Hikotai also refuelled at Naha. Unfortunately, the absence of this aircraft's entire rear section with its tail markings prevents the identification of the unit to which the Ki-49 was assigned (*Author's Collection*)

FINAL FLIGHT

Following the capitulation of Imperial Japan, announced by Emperor Hirohito on 15 August 1945, and the signing of the Japanese Instrument of Surrender on 2 September on board the battleship USS *Missouri* (BB-63) moored in Tokyo Bay, further surrender ceremonies were held by IJA and IJN units still deployed in Asia.

On 9 September, for example, Lt Gen Fusataro Teshima, commander of the IJA's 2nd Army, surrendered all Japanese forces in the eastern half of the NEI to Gen Sir Thomas A Blamey (Commander-in-Chief, Allied

The 'Helen' that transferred Gen Terashima's 2nd Army staff officers from Pinrang to Morotai was painted overall white with green crosses as per Allied surrender instructions, which also stipulated that aircraft with tail guns were to have them replaced with windsocks – as can just be seen here. This Ki-49 is a Model 2 Otsu with multiple exhausts and no spinners (*NARA*)

Land Forces, South West Pacific Area) in a special ceremony held at the sports ground of the 1st Australian Corps on Morotai. Prior to this event, Gen Teshima had had to travel by sea to Balikpapan, on Borneo, before being flown to Morotai on board an RAAF Dakota. The remaining staff officers of the 2nd Army flew from Pinrang on Celebes Island, where its headquarters was located, to Pitoe airfield on Morotai aboard a 'Sally' and a 'Helen'.

After the conclusion of the surrender ceremony, all the Japanese officers, including Teshima, flew back to Pinrang aboard the two IJAAF aircraft in order to put the surrender into effect. It was reported that it took the crew 20 minutes to get the war-weary 'Sally' started for the return journey.

IN RETROSPECT

The Donryu was not a bad aircraft per se. Nakajima had done its best to redress the shortcomings of the Ki-21 by installing self-sealing fuel tanks and giving the new design a boost in terms of its defensive armament through the fitment of 20 mm cannon in the dorsal position and, latterly, the tail turret. With the 'Sally', the forward fuselage of the bomber became quite crowded when the co-pilot/bombardier repositioned himself in that area in order to operate the bombsight, forcing him to share the already cramped space with the radio operator and the nose gunner. In the 'Helen', the relocation of the radio operator behind the two pilots was a significant improvement in the overall layout, and it allowed the crew to enjoy better in-flight communication.

However, the Ki-49 was hampered throughout its brief service life by unreliable engines. Nakajima's high-performance powerplants were notorious for not delivering their promised power outputs, and both the Ha-41 and the Ha-109 were no exception. Issues with reliability and maintenance were the most common complaints lodged by jubakutai crews. By comparison, the 'Sally's' Mitsubishi Ha-101 engines received nothing but praise from air- and groundcrew alike for being both highly reliable and easy to maintain.

Nakajima had been delivering 'Helens' from its factories for two years by the time the Ki-67 started to reach frontline units in late 1943, at which

point the Ki-49 became instantly obsolete. The 'Peggy' was the ultimate Japanese heavy bomber, with new, powerful and reliable engines, better armament and a greater top speed than even the Ki-49-III, then under development, could match. Furthermore, the Ki-67 was the only IJAAF bomber that could carry a torpedo for attacks against enemy warships – a necessary feature in the final 18 months of the war when jubakutai crews flying 'Sallys' or 'Helens' were trying in vain to sink Allied ships through skip bombing.

But even these improvements were not enough to rectify the biggest failing of all IJAAF 'heavy' bomber designs – none of them were heavy enough. 'Sallys' and 'Helens' could carry a maximum bombload of 1000-kg, while the 'Peggy' was limited to just 800-kg. The IJAAF was well aware of the B-17 Flying Fortress and its ability to carry 3600-kg of ordnance, having captured a number of airworthy examples in the Philippines in 1942 and then flight-tested them for at least two years. Yet, while the jubakutai were desperately in need of four-engined heavy bombers of the same ilk, the IJAAF remained convinced that fast attack bombers like the Ki-21, K-49 and, eventually, the Ki-67 were the best option, as they could operate closely with advancing infantry units.

When the IJA's offensive in New Guinea was stopped in late September 1942, the jubakutai were forced to fly defensive harassment missions that they had not had any training for and lacked sufficient numbers to complete with any meaningful results. The IJAAF's high command failed throughout the Pacific War to see the army air force as a separate weapon that could operate both in cooperation with the infantry but also independently of it. Simply put, the IJAAF was incapable of grasping the strategic bomber concept, remaining wedded to constricting tactical bombers. Perhaps not coincidentally, it mirrored the Luftwaffe in this respect.

While the Japanese military high command viewed the Pacific War as essentially an endless effort to capture more and more territory to prevent the enemy from using it, the Allies had a very specific goal in mind – the defeat of the Empire of Japan– and it used aircraft as the main asset to achieve this. The difference in perception between the two opposing sides reflected the way aircraft were designed and how air power was utilised. While the Allies learnt from their mistakes in the early stages of the war and sought to solve the shortcomings of their aircraft and address their tactical weaknesses, the IJAAF was fatally slow to do so.

An early production Model 1 'Helen' of the Hamamatsu school takes off on another training flight (*Author's Collection*)

The gross miscalculation to transfer all first echelon combat units to airfields considerably closer to the frontline and, therefore, enemy airfields exposed them to an endless series of unpredictable raids and resulted in the devastating August 1943 attacks that crippled the only two IJAAF jubakutai in New Guinea capable of waging offensive operations. The IJAAF failed to develop any kind of early warning system in New Guinea, even though radar was available to it, and the story was subsequently repeated at Hollandia and in the Philippines.

The allocation of forces was another area the IJAAF did not handle particularly well. The deployment of inexperienced units like the 7th and 61st Sentai, which undertook the brunt of bomber operations in New Guinea, and the 74th and 95th Sentai, which were assigned to the defence of the Philippines, resulted in poor operational effectiveness in both theatres. Conversely, the insistence on retaining the best heavy bomber sentai, like the 12th, 60th and 98th, almost permanently in Burma is a clear indication of the inflexibility of the IJAAF's High Command, which gave priority to the conclusion of the war with China by cutting off its supply routes at a time when US forces were assembling for the liberation of the Philippines.

In the final stages of the war, the IJAAF HQ had few qualms about squandering valuable bombers and their crews in ineffective suicide attacks. Much like the full frontal infantry attacks (known to the Allies as 'Banzai attacks') of World War 1, such operations were reminiscent of archaic samurai battle tactics, and had no place in modern warfare.

In the end, the massive aerial superiority of the Allies could not be matched by valiant Japanese aircrew flying an average bomber design fitted with unreliable engines. The short-sighted, inflexible and incorrigible attitude of senior officers in the IJAAF only served to make things appreciably worse.

APPENDICES

COLOUR PLATES COMMENTARY

1
Hamamatsu Rikugun Hiko Gakko (Hamamatsu Army Flying School)
The school initially used a complicated system combining fuselage and tail bands to indicate individual aircraft. The tail marking, a stylised representation of the 'ha', 'ma' and hi' elements of the school's Japanese name, changed colour to indicate the different chutai to which each aircraft belonged. Typically, these were blue for the HQ chutai, white for the 1st, red for the 2nd and yellow for the 3rd.

2
Rikugun Koku Seibi Gakko (Army Aircraft Maintenance School)
The only tail markings carried by the school's aircraft were a black stripe and individual hiragana identifiers – 'し' ('l') – on their rudders, as shown here on an early Model Ki-49.

3
Rikugun Koku Tsushin Gakko (Army Flight Radio Operators School)
The school's tail marking included a band in black and a disc in white, with an antenna and radio waves (based on the IJA military map marking symbol for an aerial radio communications unit) applied to the latter also in black.

4
11th Hikoshidan Shireibu Hikohan (11th Air Division Headquarters Flight)
This unit was formed on 17 July 1944 in Osaka and assigned to the defence of the region, operating a variety of aircraft including fighters. This Donryu was probably used as a transport, the chrysanthemum-based marking on its tail being retained from its previous unit, the 18th Hikodan Shireibu (Air Brigade HQ), which disbanded the same day the 11th Hikoshidan Shireibu Hikohan was formed.

5
Ki-49 Model 2 Ko of the 61st Sentai, 2nd Chutai, Hollandia, New Guinea, April 1944

This artwork depicts the Ki-49 Model 2 Ko found destroyed at Hollandia airfield in April 1944. It sports a rough, rather unusual camouflage consisting of random green 'Xs' applied to the bomber's overall natural metal finish. The tail marking has been incorrectly identified in the past as belonging to the 7th Sentai. The information presented in this publication for the first time, combined with supporting photographic evidence, clearly proves that it actually belonged to the 61st Sentai – the marking is a combination of the Roman numerals VI (6) and I (1).

6
Hollandia, April 1944

The colour photographs on this page feature a number of different types of IJAAF aircraft found wrecked at Hollandia airfield by the Allies following its capture in April 1944. Among the types visible is a Ki-46 'Dinah', Ki-61 'Tony', Tachikawa Type LO Transport Aircraft, codenamed 'Thelma' (a licence-built copy of the Lockheed Model 14 Super Electra), and at least two Ki-49 'Helen' bombers belonging to the 20th Independent Chutai. (*both © Jeffrey Ethell Collection*)

7
Ki-49 Model 2 Otsu of the 20th Independent Chutai, Hollandia, April 1944

This artwork depicts one of the Model 2 Otsu featured in the colour photographs of the previous page. The 20th Independent Chutai was formed on 15 May 1943 from the Teishin Hiko (Paratrooper Transport) Sentai with nine Ki-57 'Topsy' transport aircraft and 78 personnel. It was active in the Solomons, New Guinea, the NEI and the Philippines. Apart from the Ki-57s, the unit received a small number of 'Helens' left behind by heavy bomber sentai formerly in-theatre, and it flew them on transport missions in New Guinea. The 20th was disbanded on 30 May 1945. The unit's marking consisted of a numeral 2 inside a circle, symbolising the number 20. This particular aircraft sports a heavily applied madara (mottled) green camouflage over a natural metal finish.

8
Wakde Island, May 1944

This Ki-49 Model 2 from the 61st Sentai was found heavily damaged by US forces after the capture of Wakde Island (Wakde actually consists of two islands – Insumuar, the larger of the two on which the airfield was located, and Insumanai, which is much smaller) during Operation *Straight Line* in May 1944. The bomber was camouflaged with green squiggle patterns applied on an overall hairyokushoku (greyish green) finish. It had no tail marking, so the aircraft was probably an attrition replacement. Groundcrew assigned to the 61st Sentai had little time to apply tail markings to new aircraft in the frenetic final stages of the battle for West New Guinea. (*© Jeffrey Ethell Collection*)

9, 10 and 11
Del Carmen airfield, the Philippines, 1945

These three colour photographs feature a destroyed Ki-49 Model 2 Otsu that was found by US forces north of Del Carmen airfield in 1945. The bomber belonged to the 74th Sentai, 2nd Chutai, its 'Iron Cross'-like unit marking representing a 'four sevens' take on the unit number. (*all © Jeffrey Ethell Collection*)

12
Ki-49 Model 2 Otsu of the 74th Sentai, 2nd Chutai, Del Carmen airfield, the Philippines, 1944–45

This artwork depicts the Ki-49 Model 2 Otsu featured in the colour photographs on the previous page. The uppersurfaces of the aircraft were painted in a three-colour (green, mustard yellow and brown) camouflage pattern applied to some 'Helens' based in Manchuria – this Ki-49 was probably an attrition replacement flown to the Philippines from there. Its undersurfaces were painted in hairyokushoku.

13
Ki-49 Model 2 Otsu of the 74th Sentai, 2nd Chutai, the Philippines, October 1944

The 74th Sentai received orders to advance from its base in Hokkaido to the Philippines in October 1944. Some of the unit's aircraft, including this Ki-49, were equipped with Taki-1 search radar for maritime patrol missions. Note the lack of propeller spinners. The aircraft's uppersurfaces were camouflaged with an even finish of green paint over natural metal. The red and yellow marking on the side of the nose gunner's position probably indicated that this aircraft was equipped with radar.

14
Ki-49 Model 2 Otsu of an unknown unit, Nichols Field, the Philippines, 1945

This near-complete Ki-49 Model 2 Otsu devoid of unit markings was found by US personnel in February 1945 when they liberated Nichols Field (present-day Ninoy Aquino International Airport) in southern Manila. (*both © Jeffrey Ethell Collection*)

15
Ki-49 Model 2 Otsu of the 95th Sentai, 1st Chutai, Clark Field, the Philippines, late 1944

This Model 2 Otsu of the 95th Sentai is depicted in typical late-war camouflage, with almost solid green uppersurfaces. The 95th was the only IJAAF Ki-49 unit never to adopt a tail marking, choosing instead to apply a slanting band on the rear fuselage immediately behind the standard combat stripe. While the later was always white, the former could be white, red or yellow to indicate the 1st, 2nd or 3rd Chutai, respectively.

16
Ki-49 of an unknown unit, Nichols Field, the Philippines, 1945

Another wrecked Donryu at Nichols Field, photographed shortly after VJ Day. Although the bomber's tail marking is clearly visible, the insignia does not match any known IJAAF unit. (*© Jeffrey Ethell Collection*)

17
Ki-49s of an unknown unit, Yokota, Japan, 1945

These three Donryu were found abandoned at Yokota, in Kanagawa Prefecture, at war's end by occupying forces. The bomber on the left looks to be in overall natural metal finish, while the one on the right has late-war brown uppersurface camouflage. The essentially complete example in the middle has green camouflage paint applied over its overall grey finish. No tail markings are visible on any of the bombers, so the unit they were assigned to remains a mystery. (*© Jeffrey Ethell Collection*)

18
Ki-49 Model 2 Ko of the 62nd Sentai, 2nd Chutai, Hamamatsu, Japan, May 1943

This Ki-49 Model 2 Ko was assigned to the 62nd Sentai at Hamamatsu just prior to the unit's relocation from Japan to Malaya and then on to Burma in the spring of 1943. The sentai adopted a tail marking featuring two stylised 6s when it converted from Ki-21s to Ki-49s, the insignia being applied in red for the 1st Chutai, white for the 2nd and yellow for the 3rd.

19
Ki-49 Model 2 Otsu, Pitoe airfield, Morotai, 9 September 1945

This aircraft, painted white overall and with green crosses added in six locations as per Allied instructions, transported staff officers of the IJA's 2nd Army to and from Morotai on 9 September 1945. They had accompanied Lt Gen Fusataro Teshima, commander of the 2nd Army, from Pinrang, on Celebes Island, in order to surrender all Japanese forces in the eastern half of the NEI to Gen Sir Thomas A Blamey in a special ceremony held on the island at the sports ground of the 1st Australian Corps. A Ki-21 in a similar scheme was also used by the surrender party.

BIBLIOGRAPHY

BOOKS

Akimoto, Minoru, *Rakkasan Butai* (Kojinsha, 2009)

Akimoto, Minoru, *All the Regular Formed Aircraft in Japanese Army* (Kantosha, 2002)

Claringbould, Michael John, *Pacific Profiles Volume Two – Japanese Army Bombers, Transports & Miscellaneous Types in New Guinea & the Solomons 1942–44* (Avonmore Books, 2020)

Francillon, René J, *Japanese Aircraft of the Pacific War* (Putnam, 1987)

Izawa, Yasuho, *Nihon Rikugun Jubakutai* (Tokuma Shoten, 1982)

Kawachiyama, Yuzuru, *Fugaku-tai no juhachinin* (Kojinsha, 2000)

Lewis, Dr Tom, *The Empire Strikes South – Japan's Air War Against Northern Australia 1942–45* (Avonmore Books, 2017)

Matsuba, Minoru, *Design With Precision No 6, World War II Twin-engined Bombers* (Kantosha, 2000)

Shores, Christopher, *Air War for Burma* (Grub Street, 2005)

Suzuki, Shoichi, *Rikugun Hiko Sentai-shi* (Sokyubanri, 1976)

Takata, Kenichi, *Sekido o Koete – Ozora no Kobo Rikugun Jubaku Sentai* (1995)

Tanaka, Kenichi, *Takachiho Koka Butai* (Hara Shobo, 1975)

Tanaka, Kenichi, *Aa Junpaku no Hana Oite* (Gakuyo Shobo, 1972)

Tanaka, Kenichi, *Ozora no Hana* (Fuyo Shobo, 1984)

Tanaka, Kenichi, *Ooinaru kake* (Gakuyo Shobo, 1978)

PERIODICALS

Senshi Sosho, various volumes, Asagumo Shinbunsha

Hiko Dai 7 Sentai no Ayumi, 1987

93 Butai Kaisoki – Hiko Dai 62 Sentai – Dai 63 Hikojo Daitai, 1980

Dai 5 Hikodan-shi – Hiko Dai 74 Sentai, Hiko Dai 95 Sentai, 1994

Tsuito – Rikugun Jubakugeki Hiko Dai 61 Sentai, 1974

Warera No Kizuna, Hiko Dai 58 Sentai Senyu-kai,

Tsubasa O Sasaete – Rikugun Shonen Kokuhei Dai 1ki Gijutsu Seito, 1986

Rikugun Koku no Chinkon Vol 1 (1978) and *Vol 2* (1982)

Model Art No 533, Nihon Rikugunki no Toso to Marking, 1999

Shohi – Rikugun Shonen Hikohei Shusshin-sha Kaiho, various issues

Tokko, various issues

Arawasi International issue No 9, April–June 2008,

Eagle Eye Series No 3, Mitsubishi Ki-21 'Sally' and Fiat BR.20 'Cicogna' in hinomaru, Arawasi, 2021

INDEX

Note: Page locators in **bold** refer to maps, pictures and illustrations.